Be An
Awesome Boss!

The Four *C*'s Model to
Leadership Success

Tim Burningham

Also by Tim Burningham

*The Wisdom Story: How to Create a High-Performing
Company Culture and Transform Results*

How Leaders Can Strengthen Their Organization's Culture

A *TAB* Original
Houston, Texas

PO BOX 5156
Houston, TX 77325

Distributed by The Awesome Boss LLC

For ordering information or special discounts for bulk purchases, please contact The Awesome Boss LLC at PO Box 5156, Houston, TX, 77325, or, betheawesomeboss@gmail.com.

Library of Congress Cataloging-In-Publication Data

Burningham, Tim.

Be an awesome boss : the four c's model to leadership success / Tim Burningham, 1st ed.
p. ; cm.

Issued also as an ebook.

ISBN: 9781095886113

1.   Leadership effectiveness. 2. Organizational culture 3. Business I. Title

Printed in the United States of America

Fourth Edition

TAB 05 17 06 09 18 20 30

Contents

*For all the leaders who have shown me
what it takes to be an awesome boss.*

Introduction

Have you ever worked for a great boss? One you knew you could count on, who cared about you, and who inspired you? What effect did this person have on your life?

Have you ever worked for a bad boss? One who drove you crazy, whom you dreaded to see, whom you knew you couldn't trust? How was your life different, working under that leader?

Over the years, I've come to realize the importance of a good boss in every worker's life.

In my career I've had the opportunity to work with many different bosses. I've observed a wide range of leadership and management styles. Some of these leaders were phenomenal managers, while many others struggled. All, or at least the vast majority, wanted to be good leaders. And of those who found leadership challenging, it wasn't that they were awful people. In fact, many of them are some of the best people I know. Yet far too many good people find it difficult to succeed as a boss. Not only does this negatively affect the individual themselves, but also it has big ramifications on the lives of those they lead and their organizations.

What if it didn't have to be this way? What if any person who desired to become a great boss could be? What if there was a simple model or framework that every leader could use to help them be successful? What if there were no more bad bosses?

I've written this book to start a tidal wave of effective leadership and to equip leaders with a model that will help them succeed.

Many studies have proved that satisfaction at work is most strongly correlated to the relationship one has with their direct supervisor—their boss. Indeed, most people do not walk away from an organization or company or even a specific job, but rather they walk away from a boss. Time and time again, I've seen good employees, valuable employees, leave an organization that needed them to stay. In my formal and informal interviews with those who have chosen to leave their companies, in many cases they didn't want to go. In most instances they would have preferred to stay. But because of their poor relationship with their direct supervisor, their boss, they felt compelled to leave.

Human capital is the most important asset for any organization in the twenty-first century. And the accessibility and ease both for candidates viewing new job opportunities and for recruiters and competitors to connect with potential candidates for their open positions have created an even greater need for companies and leaders to do all they can to retain their good people. Employees won't put up with bad bosses like they used to. They don't have to. And millions and millions of dollars are wasted by organizations around the world on the never-ending struggle of recruiting, training, and hiring new staff.

Now more than ever, it's time for companies to do all they can to retain their talented and valuable team members. Now is the time for each organization to do all it can to help its leaders become successful managers. Now more than ever, individual bosses and leaders should be searching for ways to maximize their effectiveness. Now is the time to help employees, every one, to have an amazing boss.

Whether you are the CEO of a large organization or an entry-level supervisor at a small one or anywhere in between, this book is for you. The people who work for you deserve it. You deserve it. It's time to *be an awesome boss*!

Be An
Awesome Boss!

The Four *C*'s Model to

Leadership Success

The Fable

Promotion

Martin Bremer, better known as Marty around the office and the company where he worked, had looked forward to this day since entering business school many years ago. He had worked hard, putting in long hours, even sacrificing many weekends and much personal time to get to this point in his career. Now Marty was about to become the youngest chief executive officer in Wiser Care, Inc.'s history. Though this really came as no surprise to anyone who had been with the organization for very long because of his impressive track record, what was surprising was the health care center he was chosen to lead.

Problem

For Marty, the promotion was an exciting step in his already very successful young career; however, there was one problem that dampened his enthusiasm just a little bit. Actually, it was starting to seem like a big problem to Marty. He was about to replace a Wiser Care, Inc. legend, and though he was confident he would be successful in his new role, he had to admit that his colleagues' jeers and jests about having to follow the "great" Daniel Rosier did make him a bit uneasy.

Daniel Rosier, or *Dan the Man* as most knew him, a name his direct reports had affectionately given him many years ago and still called him to this day, had run the most successful center in the company for two decades. From top awards to record numbers, Dan was seemingly on top of the world when it came to his success as a CEO at Wiser Care. He was revered and respected by his colleagues, loved and admired by his staff, and well known as one of the company's top talents and legendary heroes. Indeed, the lore of Dan Rosier was one of self-sacrifice, legendary leadership, and doing what he personally felt was best for the company in order to achieve the highest results.

After many years of service and unprecedented success, Dan was finally retiring, and Marty had been chosen as his replacement. Marty knew he had big shoes to fill. For the first time in his career, he began to feel a little uneasy, wondering whether hard work, loyalty, wit, confidence, and undeniable dedication—all things that had helped him to this point in his career—would be enough. After all, Marty had never managed an entire health care center before. Sure, he had run teams on special projects, filled in during transitions of leadership, and supervised different departments at Wiser Care's health care centers, but those opportunities were very different from this one. Marty was now becoming the ultimate decision maker as the CEO at a health care center, a thought that was both exciting and intimidating. And not everyone became a CEO at Wiser Care, Inc. The fact that Marty was given this promotion at such a young age spoke volumes about how the company viewed his worth and contribution thus far. Marty had been successful, he knew it, and now he was about to become the leader of one of the most prosperous health care centers in the entire company.

Relieved

Marty immediately felt better after hanging up the phone with Dan early Thursday morning. Dan was supposed to be leaving Friday and starting his retirement. Due to some last-minute projects and what Marty felt were unreasonable requests from his current boss, he had never had the chance to take the two-hour drive north to meet with Dan, despite the fact that he'd been promised he'd have plenty of time to spend with him before Dan left for retirement. Such was the case at Wiser Care. Operational needs and customer demands were always present. The chance to slow down and actually think was rare.

Though Marty felt he should have known better than to believe his current boss after two years of hearing false promises, he really had hoped to spend some uninterrupted time with Dan. Ever since the announcement that he was the chosen heir apparent to Dan, his hope of spending time with him had slowly grown into a salacious desire to learn all he could from him before he left. Now Marty felt angry. *And why wouldn't the company want me to shadow Dan before he was gone?* Marty thought to himself disgustedly as he analyzed his current situation. In the end he concluded this was just another example of how little his immediate boss valued and respected him and his success. This was a big reason Marty was so ready to go.

Although he had planned to leave Friday, Dan had called Marty back that afternoon, stating he had successfully convinced the company to allow him to stick around as a "volunteer" for an extra week or so in order to introduce Marty to the team and help guide him in his new role. Marty knew Dan was kidding as he had heard the reverse was true: that the company had tried to convince Dan to put off retirement for a few more years and wanted to keep him around as long as they possibly could. Nonetheless, Marty enjoyed Dan's lightheartedness, humility, and dedication to the company. More than anything, he was relieved he'd have time to spend with him.

On the phone the two leaders agreed to block out each morning of the following week so that they could spend uninterrupted time together. On the one hand, this made Marty really nervous because he knew how busy a new CEO at a health care center could be, but on the other, uninterrupted time was exactly what he had hoped for with Dan. Marty felt even better when Dan promised him he would rearrange essential meetings and talk to the team about how important it was for the two of them to have some time alone. Dan also reassured Marty by reminding him that the leadership team at the center was strong and very capable of handling concerns while they spent this time together. He then teased Marty by commenting he would be thrown into the frying pan soon enough.

On the phone Dan had also joked that Marty probably didn't need or want extra attention from an old geezer, but Marty assured him that he did. Marty could tell Dan was sincere in his desire to stick around and help him succeed, which brought a lot of relief. Truth be told, Marty wasn't typically one to ask for help or even feel like he needed it under most circumstances.

After having spoken with Dan now on two separate occasions, even if it had been for only a few minutes, he could tell there was something different about him, something genuine and intriguing that he needed to learn. Marty knew the value Dan could add to his career, and the more Marty thought about the opportunity to spend time with him, the more excited he became. Combined with his excitement, however, was some anxiety about how Dan would judge and accept him as his replacement. Would he think Marty was suitable? Would he think he was too young and inexperienced? Marty decided he couldn't worry about that. He wanted nothing more than to succeed in his new role, and he felt certain Dan could help him do just that.

The Office

As Marty walked into his new office early Monday morning, he was overwhelmed with how much room he felt it had. He tried to compose himself as he struggled to fully embrace the reality of his current situation. *I am the new CEO of this place,* he thought to himself.

Directly in front of him he noticed a large wood desk that seemed bigger than any desk he had ever seen at a Wiser Care health care center. To his left was a big open window that looked out to some nice landscaping on the side of the building. He also noticed a small table with two chairs neatly nestled next to the window, through which the sunlight was currently shining through. In front of the large desk were two plush, padded brown chairs, and back behind the desk in each of the far corners of the office were tall bookshelves that went nearly all the way to the high ceiling. As Marty continued to look around his new office, he also noticed a big whiteboard on the wall next to the door and another much smaller desk and chair on the other side of the door. Marty tried to take it all in as the excitement of the day ratcheted up to a whole new level for him.

The CEO's office felt big and powerful. Marty felt a sense of pride and accomplishment wash over him. It was exhilarating yet frightening at the same time. As he continued to look around the office, feelings of freedom came—freedom from the "do as you're told and don't ask questions" mentality he'd felt most of his former supervisors always had toward him, not to mention the closet-size offices he often found himself working out of the past nine years at Wiser Care. If he was honest with himself, Marty hadn't really enjoyed his career to this point— the long hours, the extra projects, and sacrificing so much just to try and please his bosses, who either didn't seem to care all that much or never seemed satisfied and always demanded more. It wasn't an easy road. His wife and young daughter could attest to that as they also had felt the effects of the challenges Marty faced at work along the way. *It all has finally paid off*, he thought. He had the feeling that he had finally arrived as he placed a box of his personal belongs on the small empty desk next to the door.

Marty also quickly noticed Dan had cleaned out most of his belongings. Though this was to be expected, he felt a little bit of sadness that he hadn't seen what the office had looked like beforehand. It also was a stirring reminder to Marty that Dan really was leaving and that he was now going to be fully in charge of the decisions, direction, and results at the center.

Marty had been so focused on his plans for his new role that he was surprised when he momentarily allowed his mind to wander and think about the far-off day when he, too, would be retiring. "It must feel nice, packing up and heading off to a good, relaxing retirement after so many years of sweat, grind, and success," Marty said out loud to himself.

The impressive nature of his new office and these thoughts of retirement didn't last long. Marty's mind quickly turned back to all the work that lay ahead of him and the things he knew he needed to do to live up to a legend and be successful as a CEO. Though he had already made quite the name for himself, he recognized there was still a lot of work for him to do in order to permanently leave his mark on Wiser Care and prove he belonged with the Daniel Rosiers of the company. Marty was competitive by nature and wanted nothing more.

After a few minutes of being alone in his office, he heard a knock at his door that was cracked open. Before he could say anything, his executive assistant, Kate, peeked her head in ever so slightly. Marty knew that Kate was a relatively new member to the team and had worked with Dan for about a year. He noticed she was a middle-aged woman with short dark hair. Dan had praised Kate during one of his phone conversations with Marty, calling her a lifesaver. He said she was known for always being on top of things. Kate, however, seemed different from how Marty thought she might be based on Dan's description of her. After Marty invited her in, she timidly walked into his office and introduced herself. Marty realized she was nervous. Though he was surprised that Kate seemed nervous around him, he remembered how he often felt around a new boss. He was certain this leadership transition wouldn't be easy for her or for most of the leaders at the center. He hoped he could make it as smooth as possible for all of them. After his brief conversation with Kate, he decided he'd really like working with her. Marty had a feeling he was going to enjoy his new role as *the boss*.

Surprises

A few minutes later Dan walked into the office with his arm around a gentleman who was holding a small broom and dustpan in his right hand. Dan was gray-haired, tall, thin, and a little younger looking than Marty expected, and the man with him was an older, tall, and slender gentleman who wore what looked like a housekeeper uniform. Dan quickly introduced the man to Marty with a big smile, and Marty shook the man's hand. Marty learned his name was Roger, and he had worked at the health care center almost as long as Dan had. Dan and Roger spoke again for a few minutes like old friends, which surprised Marty, and then Roger hurried off back to work. Dan then turned to Marty again with another contagious smile and asked, "Well, what do you think?" with his arms stretched out wide.

"I love it," Marty said, trying to hide how much he truly did love his new office. Marty shook his colleague's hand and exchanged pleasantries with him for a few minutes, taking care to express his excitement over the opportunity to learn from him. Dan congratulated Marty on his new position and shared how impressed he was with all Marty had done thus far in his career at Wiser Care. He also assured him he would be great in this new role. Marty really appreciated Dan's kind words.

After a minute or two of this small talk, Dan said to Marty, "Well, should we sit down?" and extended his arm toward the two brown chairs positioned neatly in front of the large wooden desk.

Marty replied, "Sure," as he sat down in one of the comfortable chairs. As he did, he couldn't help but think, *These are mine!* That thought, however, was quickly chased away.

Dan turned to Marty with a thoughtful look on his face and said in a very serious voice, "Don't be like everyone else, Marty. Please, I beg you, don't do it. That's a sure way to fail."

Marty was instantly surprised. "Like everyone else?" he quietly questioned, unsure of what Dan was talking about. The seriousness of Dan's demeanor was so different from the way he had acted on the phone and up to this point that Marty felt a little nervous as Dan's big brown eyes seemed to penetrate him. He wasn't sure what to expect next.

Dan then continued without really answering Marty's question. "I'd like to teach you something very important to me that I know will help you be successful in your new role. In fact, I'm so confident that if you follow what I am about to tell you, I can almost guarantee your success as a big boss," Dan said with a slight smile, now easing back in his chair. Marty felt Dan had probably noticed his wide eyes and tense posture, so he tried to relax a bit as well. "I didn't always live by what I am about to share with you, Marty," Dan continued, "and I got in trouble for it. But since I began to do my best at following this model, my life has never been the same."

As Dan spoke, Marty's eyes opened wide again, and his eyebrows raised as he said, "This is exactly what I want to know!" Marty knew he had a tendency to get excited quickly and let his emotions get the best of him at times, so he did his best to conceal the exhilaration that he was now feeling. *I need to know Dan's secret to success!* he thought to himself.

Although Marty wasn't sure what Dan was about to tell him, he recognized going into this meeting that Dan clearly knew things that others didn't seem to know. *How else could he be so successful for so long throughout his career?* Marty reasoned to himself. The health care industry was always changing and as a result was full of short-tenure leaders and high turnover. The fact that Dan had lasted at Wiser Care, Inc. for as long as he had was incredible. Even more, the fact that he had managed to stay put and have success at the same health care center for two decades was almost unheard of.

Though he had never verbalized it to anyone, Marty had wondered how much Dan would really share with him. His experiences in the past had taught him that many successful leaders liked to keep things to themselves, but at that moment Marty was certain Dan was willing to share it all. He also believed that what Dan was about to share with him would be big and could send him down the road to legendary status at Wiser Care. Whatever it was that Dan was about to say, Marty was ready to hear it and embrace it, or at least he thought he was.

"I want to share with you four *C*'s that will keep you from being a bad boss," Dan said, looking a little more serious again and sitting up in his chair.

Marty had contemplated a lot about what Dan might share with him prior to their meeting. Perhaps he'd share the most critical key metrics and reports he needed to keep an eye on and always drive. Or maybe how to decipher which service niches to offer and promote. Or maybe how to win over customers or keep key relationships in place in order to maintain high census and service volume. Though it took a moment, Marty realized his ideas could not have been any further from what Dan had just said.

Marty tried to minimize his body's automatic reaction to the surprise he felt. His mind was trying to compute where this conversation was going when Dan moved his eyes up above

Marty, then turned his head slightly as if pondering his next words.

Finally, Dan blew out some air, crossed his arms, and said, "Marty, tell me something. How many bosses have you had during your career?"

Marty thought for a minute, a little unsure of why Dan was asking, then replied, "I've had five immediate supervisors I've reported to here at Wiser Care."

"And how many of those bosses would you say acted like..." Dan paused for a moment as if he was trying to find the right words before continuing. "Well, like they were in over their heads, for lack of a better phrase?"

From all accounts, Dan was an extremely polished and professional executive, and now Marty was completely shocked by where the conversation was going. He again tried to hide his automatic emotional response to what he had just heard. As he carefully contemplated the best way to answer the question, Dan thankfully broke the silence.

"Excuse my poor choice of words," Dan said, shaking his head slightly. Marty thought Dan probably noticed his look of surprise. "Now, I don't mean 'in over their heads' like they were unintelligent or incapable of doing a good job, but what I mean to say is, have you ever felt like your boss maybe shouldn't have become a boss? Like perhaps they were in the wrong role? Or have you felt maybe they didn't seem to grasp how they could be a good boss? Or if they did understand it, they didn't seem to really apply the principles of what generally makes a great boss?"

Marty thought about how he had struggled with many of his bosses up to this point, and one in particular had really driven him crazy while he worked under him. In fact, Marty still held bitter feelings toward him to this day. Though each boss Marty had had was different, he felt for the most part in general they were unfair and jealous, hard-nosed and hypocritical, and uncaring and inconsiderate. And in truth, because of many of them, Marty had not enjoyed his career all that much. This is one major reason why Marty had worked extra hard so that one day he would not have to answer to one of these...well, bad bosses.

And there it was. Marty *did* think most were in over their heads. Though he had never really thought about it in that way, it didn't take long for him to realize it. He had always felt deep down inside that once he was leading a health care center himself, he wouldn't have to deal with what he called an inept boss. And although he did think his prior bosses were all in over their heads in some way, he knew better than to openly and carelessly admit it.

"Well, I don't know if I'd say they were in over their heads, but perhaps they all had some different ways about them that sometimes made things a little more challenging for me and others than maybe they had to be," Marty responded carefully, quickly adding, "but I'm sure they did the best they could."

Through the years, Marty had learned to play well the seemingly tireless corporate game. He knew to be guarded and careful when speaking about others, especially your superiors. You never knew when someone might use your words against you or throw you under the bus just to help themselves get ahead or to make your life miserable. Marty didn't believe it would be wise if he opened up completely and shared his true feelings about his previous bosses with Dan at this time. The truth was, however, that Marty had almost quit many times because of the seeming incompetence and uncaring nature of many of his prior supervisors. The last thing Marty wanted to do right now, though, was to leave a bad impression with Dan. For all he knew, Dan had spoken with Marty's previous bosses—at the very least, he certainly was well connected with many leaders throughout the organization.

"I see," Dan said, looking again as if he wasn't sure how to express his next thought. All of a sudden, he looked Marty straight in the eye and bluntly stated, "I'm not sure how else to say this, Marty, but to be frank with you, I worry that eighty-five percent of the bosses at Wiser Care—in fact, probably in most of the world—are not very good bosses, including those you may have worked under, and it's not necessarily their fault." Marty was again surprised by Dan's candor as he continued, "Throughout my career I've met and worked with a lot of bosses, and I don't want you to become one of them. I want you to be different, Marty. I want you to be a good boss. One who leads in a way where people look up to you, respect you, and believe in you. A boss your people know they can count on. The people at Wiser Care deserve that; my people here in this health care center deserve it. Everyone deserves an awesome boss."

Marty listened closely, trying to understand what Dan was saying. Obviously, he wanted to be a good boss and had vowed long ago not to be like the majority of the bosses he had worked under, but he didn't exactly know where Dan was going with all this. *Is this it? Is this the big secret? Is Dan's advice to simply try to be a good boss?,* Marty thought. It seemed so obvious and so intangible. Marty wanted something he could do, something he could focus on, something he had never heard before, and certainly something more concrete. He felt a little uneasy as he moved uncomfortably in his chair and waited to hear what Dan would say next.

"The thing is, many bosses are really good people and, other than a very small minority, truly want to be good bosses. Very few leaders, I believe, wake up and say, 'I want to be a really crummy boss for my people today. I don't want them to enjoy

19

where they work or who they work for.' That isn't it at all."
Marty slowly nodded, agreeing, as Dan continued, "I hope you
don't misunderstand what I'm saying. Many people who
become bosses could be highly successful; however, they lack
some good guidance and understanding of what matters most
to being a good boss. They lack a model that could inform their
decision-making and guide their behavior and actions—that
could point them to things that really have an impact and that
would result in their success as a leader."

Though still perplexed by the unexpected topic of their
conversation, Marty suddenly found himself feeling a bit more
intrigued about what Dan might say next.

The Four *C*'s Model

"Marty, I want to share with you what I call *The Four C's Model to Leadership Success*, which I believe will help you avoid becoming like the majority of bosses in the workplace. I can promise you that if you successfully implement these four *C*'s, or at least do them to the best of your ability, and get others on your leadership team to help you establish them throughout the center I might add, you'll get the most out of your people, and you'll feel good about doing it."

It appeared to Marty that Dan was now becoming surer of what he wanted to say, though he was still trying to wrap his mind around where the conversation was going.

"What I'm about to share isn't necessarily a big mystery or even new concepts. It's quite obvious, really. However, the elements in the four *C*'s model often don't get the attention they need. And too many leaders don't fully appreciate their impact and significance. For this reason, though the concepts in the four *C*'s model are simple, they provide a powerful framework for leadership success. Having the model reminds leaders just how important these concepts are, especially when working together. The four elements within the model, or the four *C*'s, are too important to not take seriously, Marty. Don't let the simplicity of what I'm about to share with you distract you from how important each element is to your eventual success."

Not a big mystery? Simple? If Marty was honest with himself, this news was a little bit of a disappointment and not at all what he'd expected to hear from Dan today. Rather than show any signs of discouragement, though, he looked at Dan and said, "I'm all ears," encouraging him to continue.

"I believe most leaders know and understand at some level the importance of each of the four *C*'s, yet they still mostly fail to do them. And I have my theories on why this is, but we won't get into that now," Dan said, smiling. "What I can say, though, is that because they fail to focus on the four *C*'s, often their people are unhappy and frustrated at work. And when people don't feel good about work, then performance and results are always less than what they ought to be. Frankly, people deserve better. They deserve a good boss—even an amazing boss. People should be happy at work and feel good about who they work for. So much of that here at this center now depends on you."

Marty was a little astonished. Though he knew his role was important, he had never fully considered how much of an impact he might have on other people's lives as a CEO. He began to wonder why he had never considered this since his previous bosses had definitely had a big impact on his life.

Marty also began to wonder how the four *C*'s would help him keep everyone satisfied. Though this was not at all what Marty had expected from Dan, he was becoming more fascinated by it all. He also felt his level of admiration growing for Dan. He could see Dan was passionate about what he was sharing and believed in it wholeheartedly. And based on Dan's track record of incredible results, he must surely know what he was talking about, Marty reminded himself. At this point Marty already had a lot of questions, but he decided it would be best to wait for Dan to explain further rather than interrupt his momentum.

"During the next four mornings, I'd like to tell you about the four C's, focusing on one each day. I promise I'll just take a few hours of your time each morning and then allow you to do some real work," Dan added with a smile. "I have to warn you that it hasn't been easy implementing each element; it takes continuous effort. However, I've spent many years at this center trying to establish each of them, and, well...you can see the results for yourself." Dan looked at Marty in the eyes for a moment and then looked down. Although Marty could tell Dan was very confident in what he was sharing, he also didn't feel any sense of arrogance or bragging. This was another reason Marty was intrigued by Dan and another way he seemed different from many of the other CEOs he had met in the company.

Dan looked up again. "Now, Marty, as you make a conscious effort as a leader to create each element within your center, you'll be more successful than you otherwise would be. If you fail to focus on the elements in the model, you'll be like most other bosses out there who struggle. Without a focus on these four C's, you won't get the results you hope for, and you most likely won't lead in a way that is inspiring. I know how much there is to do around here, and I know it will be a sacrifice to give up your mornings and dedicate them to learning the four C's model, but if you are up for it, I think it will be well worth your time. I'm thoroughly convinced the four C's model is at the heart of all leadership success."

Marty knew he couldn't say anything other than yes. He knew this was a chance to learn from one of the best at Wiser Care, Dan the Man, and he could tell he was very serious about it. However, he also couldn't help wondering if this was really what he needed to learn most of all from him. *Aren't there possibly even more important things to know about other than the four C's thing?* Marty sensed that Dan didn't think so, so he quickly pushed those thoughts aside, reasoning that if his career could turn out anything like Dan's, he'd be thrilled. And although he did worry about everything he had to do or wanted to do in his health care center right away, he believed Dan when he said it would be worth his time. So no matter the sacrifice of time needed to learn the four C's thing that Dan seemed so sure about, Marty felt ready.

"The last thing I'll say before we get to the model is that I didn't always follow it because it wasn't always clear in my mind. The model is something I've pieced together over my career. I've seen way too many good people fail as a boss over my years, and this had caused me to reflect on why that was and why my results turned out different from theirs. The model comes from many years of experience, observation, and practice. What I have learned in sharing this model with others is that in every situation, no matter the size or scope of the team, or the strengths and weaknesses of the leader, or even the industry, this model works when rigorously applied. And it will work for you."

Marty's curiosity was now at an all-time high.

"Before I share the first C, I want you to know that all the C's fit together and build on each other. They produce a model for effective leadership and effective organizational cultures. They work together and support and build on each other. When you focus on each of them properly, it will help you achieve impressive results as a leader."

Marty loved the sound of that and leaned forward in his seat, ready to hear more.

"So," Dan said with some excitement in his voice. "Are you ready to learn about the first C?"

Marty nodded eagerly as the moment hit him. He couldn't believe he was going to learn a leadership model from the man he had heard so much about over the last nine years while working at Wiser Care. Within the company, Dan was the definition of incredible leadership and stellar results. Marty had high hopes the four *C's* model could help him create his own legacy.

Part One

Clarity

The First *C*

"OK, Marty," Dan said. "The first *C* of the model stands for 'clarity.'"

Though Marty wasn't really sure what he was expecting, he felt a little let down from the high he had just been experiencing after the disclosure of the first *C*. *Clarity?* he thought to himself. *What does that have to do with anything?* Marty was thoroughly confused by the first *C*, and he noticed Dan could tell.

"You look less than thrilled by this," Dan said honestly, adding, "and that's OK. Let me try and explain just how important this is to you as a leader. Do you mind if I use that?" Dan pointed to the whiteboard at the far side of the office.

"Sure," Marty said, trying to recover again. He felt a little guilty that Dan recognized he was not ecstatic about the revelation of the first *C*, but he wasn't sure what to say at this point. Luckily, Dan stood and walked quickly over to the whiteboard, which gave Marty a moment to recover.

Dan picked a marker from the few scattered on the ledge of the whiteboard and wrote:

Then he placed the marker down and began to speak as he walked back to the chair positioned across from Marty. "Let me ask you something. Now, I know you're a lot younger than me, but have you ever had to watch something on TV that wasn't very clear? Like maybe there was a storm outside or something was affecting the signal, so the images weren't coming in very clear on the screen?"

It brought to mind watching the Super Bowl last year during a massive snowstorm that had hit the Northeast. "Yes, I guess so," Marty replied.

"What was that like?" Dan now asked.

"It made me pretty upset. Just when something exciting was about to happen, the TV would cut off and then back on, and I'd miss a big play. Other times the screen was so blurry, it was hard to even follow the ball and know if a pass from the quarterback had been caught, dropped, or intercepted." Though he was speaking, Marty still didn't quite understand where Dan was going with this.

"Exactly!" said Dan, more excited than Marty expected. "Not having clarity can make us pretty upset; that's a great way to put it. We like to know what is going on, and we like to be able to see clearly. Not seeing clearly or not knowing what is going on causes frustration and confusion. It can make us pretty upset."

Marty nodded as he tried to fully grasp what Dan was saying.

"Like the frustration you felt during your experience with the fuzzy TV, the people you lead and who work for you want to see clearly. They want to know if a pass here at work is caught or dropped. Without knowing, the game just isn't very enjoyable."

Clarity makes work more enjoyable? Marty thought about that for a moment and could see Dan's point. He could agree to a certain extent that clarity would help someone feel more informed and part of the team.

Marty, feeling more interested in where this conversation was going, wanted to understand better, so he asked, "I'm not sure I know exactly what you mean. Can you *clarify*?" He drew out the word *clarify* with a little bit of a smirk on his face. Marty was known for being someone who liked to joke around from time to time. This was his first attempt at making Dan laugh. He wasn't sure how he'd react.

"Nice one," Dan said with what seemed like a gracious chuckle. Then he added, "I'd love to make this *clearer* for you." He overemphasized the word. Marty liked his playful response and could tell Dan wasn't always as intense as he had seemed for most of the morning thus far.

Dan then continued. "The people who work for you crave clarity. All of us do. We want to know what the game is all about, what we're trying to accomplish as a team, and what the plan is. We all want to know what role we are expected to play and how we can benefit the team. And we all want to know why we're doing what we're doing and how it helps us and others. When these things are made crystal clear, your people will work with less frustration, confusion, and undue stress. They will be able to focus on what matters most, and they'll enjoy the game, or their work, so much more."

"OK, I think I can buy that," Marty said. It was starting to make more sense to him. He thought clarity did seem important, but was it really that big of a deal? Marty hoped he wouldn't be disappointed with what Dan had to say next.

Building Blocks

Dan stood and stretched for a moment, saying, "Don't ever get old, Marty; this back is killing me."

Marty smiled and said, "Would you like to switch seats, or can I get you a different chair?"

"No, this is the best chair we've got. Trust me, I know; I've tried every chair in this place." Marty had to smile at that thought when Dan added, "I'll be fine if you don't mind me stretching and moving around every once in a while."

"That's completely fine by me," Marty replied.

Dan then sat back down and said, "Without clarity at work, everything slows down. People have to fill in the gaps, which leads to confusion, frustration, and unproductive disagreements. Painting a clear picture for people is what exceptional bosses do, while less-than-stellar bosses don't pay much attention to it at all."

Marty realized he hadn't necessarily paid much attention to clarity in his positions in the past. As he thought about it, though, he realized he did try to keep everyone informed and moving in the same direction. Maybe clarity had played a bigger role in his success than he realized.

Breaking Marty away from his thoughts, Dan continued, "You know, I believe most team members at Wiser, and probably in most companies around the world, want to do a good job. I truly believe this is inherent in each of us, but not knowing how to do a good job or what a good job looks like or even why a good job is important makes things unnecessarily difficult and confusing. Like you said with the blurry TV, it can be pretty upsetting."

Marty was listening closely now to what Dan was saying. He was starting to really feel there was more to clarity than he may have realized as Dan went on, "Think about the anxiety that comes from people worrying about whether they're doing a good job or whether they're doing what their boss wants them to do. Leaders who can create clarity around what is most important and what a good job looks like will get better results from their people because they won't be worrying all the time."

"OK, I get your point, but I don't understand exactly what"—Marty hesitated, not wanting to offend Dan. He could see Dan was serious about this. And he already had a lot of respect for him, so he decided to slow down and continue cautiously, trying not to sound too skeptical—"a boss needs to make clear. I mean, it seems for the most part things are somewhat clear, and this doesn't seem to affect performance all that much." Marty knew his last comment sounded a little too incredulous as a quick, almost undiscernible frown came to Dan's face. He then furrowed his brow as if he were thinking.

"OK, this is a great question you bring up," Dan said, looking more thoughtful now, adding, "and I hope I can do a better job at explaining why the first *C* is so important. It's the base of our model—the foundation of successful leadership." Dan leaned forward again in his chair and said, "High levels of clarity are essential for becoming a great boss and establishing a healthy culture among your team. Though performance may be good, high levels of clarity can make performance great."

Dan now sat tall in his chair, as if trying to maneuver in a way so that his back wouldn't bother him so much. "Now, to answer your question about what a boss needs to make clear, the simple answer is everything." Marty didn't love the ambiguous answer, but Dan quickly explained. "You see, as a good boss, one of your number-one priorities should be providing clarity on everything you possibly can. You can never make things too clear. I've never heard anyone say to a boss, 'Well, you made that much clearer than it needed to be,' especially around the most important things."

Marty chuckled at that thought and agreed; however, he wondered what the most important things were.

"I'm not talking about micromanaging here or dictating what everyone should be doing at any given moment during their day. That would be as impossible as it would be ridiculous. So that isn't it at all. Good clarity around things that matter most actually leads to less of a need to micromanage. Clarity empowers your team to act and gives you the peace of mind that they will act in a way that is aligned and will help your results."

Marty thought about that for a moment, and then Dan added, "You need to give clear direction, and leaders should try to be as clear as possible on everything they can. However, there are three things that are the most important that every great leader must make sure are clear. I call these the building blocks."

Dan suddenly stood up, walked back toward the whiteboard, and wrote:

Building Blocks
- Mission
- Vision
- Values

He then turned and said, "Marty, the most important things you need to make clear are your mission, vision, and values."

Dan then walked back to the chair and sat down with more of a plop this time. Marty wondered if his back was feeling better when Dan smiled and said, "A good mission and vision provide purpose. They answer the important question of why. And values provide behavioral expectations. They inform people how you expect them to act.

"When these are clear, you don't have to hold people's hands; they'll know what's expected of them and what the purpose is. They will make decisions based on them. Establishing clarity around these most important items will make your job much easier as a boss."

Dan stopped now, and Marty could tell he was trying to decide whether Marty was following what he was saying. Marty wanted to show he was listening, so he sat up in his chair, nodding his head.

Dan seemed to take the cue and continued. "Like seeing a clear picture on a TV removes frustration, your people need to understand what the team is trying to accomplish and where it's heading. They also need to know clearly why they wake up every day and come to work for you. They need to know what the point of all the effort is. These are all things your mission and vision should answer. And this is why it is so important that these building blocks are clear. When your people don't know the point of their work, where they're going, or what values they stand for, it's hard for them to get very excited about work. Everyone from top to bottom in our health care center here must know these building blocks. They must come to work with purpose."

"OK, I see how this would be meaningful." Marty responded sincerely now.

"Good," Dan said with a slight smile. "Let's start now with the mission. In our center we don't come to work every day just to do a job or collect a paycheck, but we come on a mission. This is the reason for our work. Our mission defines what we're trying to accomplish each day we wake up and come here. Every day, each one of us is on a mission; we all have the same purpose," Dan said, emphasizing his point.

Marty wondered if all the staff at the center truly felt like they had a clearly defined purpose for their work as Dan was suggesting. Sure, every center where Marty had worked had had a mission statement, but it honestly wasn't talked about much, and Marty wasn't sure it gave anyone much purpose. While Marty thought about this, Dan continued, "If you ask any of my staff..." He stopped for a second as if he had misspoken and said, "Sorry, I mean, if you ask any of *your* staff out there why they come to work each day, I bet you they'll all respond the same. They may not use the exact same words, but they'll be very close. This is because of our emphasis on clarity. There is clarity among the team here about our health care center's mission. We share a common purpose. We've worked hard to make it clear to all."

Marty raised his eyebrows a bit hearing this, but he could tell Dan didn't seem to mind. He imagined Dan had seen skeptical looks before while sharing this information.

Dan continued. "My people..." Marty noticed Dan hesitate again, catching himself. "I mean, *your* people have to know why they do what they do. I'm telling you, Marty, they all know it here. No one wakes up and gets ready for work without knowing why around here. We all come to work for the same reason, the same purpose, the same *mission*. Every one of your team members knows it. They know the purpose of their work each day."

Marty sat still in his chair. *Could every single staff member at the center really recite the purpose or mission if asked?* After contemplating this question for a second, Marty quietly whispered to himself, "Incredible." He thought about the many other centers he had worked at. He knew for a fact that very few employees at each center could respond with what the actual mission was for their center. In fact, he had to admit to himself that he probably couldn't have recited the mission statement most of the time, and he was in management. Based on what Dan was saying, he could see how this might be important.

"Do you remember Roger, whom I introduced you to a little while ago?" Dan asked, leaning back in his chair again.

"You mean the friendly-looking housekeeper?" Marty questioned, wondering if he was the right person.

"Yes, Roger, the man who always makes us look good," Dan said with a smile, nodding his head. "Not that this should surprise you, but Roger comes to work each day on a mission, and it shows in his work," Dan said proudly. "It wasn't always that way, though. When he first began here, Roger wasn't happy, and anyone could tell. I learned pretty quickly he viewed his job as one that had little value and that served only as a way to put some food on the table for his family.

"However, that all changed many years ago. When we introduced our mission and vision, our 'why' here at the center, and continually talked about it and reinforced that we were serious about it, things changed for him. Roger more than most really internalized why we were doing what we were doing here, and it just made the difference for him. He's embraced our purpose for years, and I've observed him truly trying each day to create excellent experiences for each person he meets. He gets it," Dan said now with emphasis. "He even teaches others when they join us. I believe this is one reason he does such a good job around here and works so hard to make this place look great. But it wasn't always that way."

Marty sat back and was considering what Dan had just shared when he added, "And the magic here at this center is that every team member does the same because the purpose is clear. No one, not even Roger, has to wonder what our purpose is here at our health care center or what they should be trying to do. We all together are striving toward the same purpose each day. We are united in that way."

Marty leaned back farther in his chair now, putting his hands behind his head as he tried to soak in this information. He had to admit he was still surprised by what Dan was saying. Though it seemed a little strange to consider Roger coming to work on a mission each day, Marty realized that by doing so, he probably felt his work was important and felt good about the contributions he was making. In fact, this simple idea was beginning to feel momentous to Marty. *If every employee were working toward the same clear purpose each day, it would have a real impact on results*, Marty thought. *Not to mention how it might help teamwork and camaraderie.* Marty considered the implications of an entire team being clear about their shared purpose. He then made a mental note to ask Roger what he felt his mission was the next time he saw him. Not that he didn't believe Dan, but Marty had to put what he was saying to the test.

"The mission defines why you and your team come to work every day. It provides a clear purpose for your daily work." Dan looked at Marty as if he wanted to make sure he understood. Marty leaned forward again, placing his hands in front of him, nodding.

"The vision informs people where the company is going, what it is destined for, and the contribution it hopes to make to the world," Dan slowly continued. Marty could tell he was still trying to make sure he was grasping what he was saying when he added, "Without a clear vision, it can be hard to get excited about work because you don't know where you are going. A vision is like a destination, and without a clear destination, your team might take you and the organization anywhere. Who knows where you might end up," Dan said, shrugging his shoulders. Marty thought about that, and it made sense.

"The final building block is your values. Your values are the important behavioral expectations you have for your team— they inform people how they ought to behave. Most people want to act how you'd like them to. They want to know what behaviors are valued and expected. If you make these very clear, they will strive to live up to them."

Dan then stood again and, pointing to the board at the far end of the room, stated, "These first items, the building blocks, work together. Your values should help your people live the mission day in and day out, and living your mission should help you achieve your vision. These are the most crucial things you must make clear. When you're clear around these most important items, they'll guide the decision-making for your entire team. When you establish clarity on them, meaning everyone knows what they are and understands them, you set the stage for great results."

At that moment Marty completely forgot about the feelings of doubt and disappointment he'd had earlier that morning when Dan revealed the first *C*. Marty could see the conviction Dan had about what he was saying, and his thoughts turned to all the lore and accomplishments Dan and his health care center had achieved. *Could clarity around these items really be the cause for his success?* Marty knew he better start trusting Dan more completely.

Big-Ticket Items

Still standing, Dan stretched again for a minute and then walked back to the whiteboard. Before he picked up a pen, he stopped and said, "There's more you should strive to make clear as a boss, Marty. These," he said, pointing to the board, "are the first and most important. These building blocks are a must. They must be the highest on your clarity priority list. But there are other items that are critical as well. I call these big-ticket items, for lack of a better term. Clarity around these big-ticket items should also be a high priority. And though these are the best places to start when it comes to clarity, the goal should still be to provide as much clarity and openness around everything you possibly can. However, I will say that when these building blocks and big-ticket items are clear, people can perform at their best."

Dan then added this to the board:

Building Blocks
- Mission
- Vision
- Values

Big-Ticket Items
- Roles & Responsibilities
- Evaluation Process
- Standards & Expectations
- Goals
- Results
- "The Why" (for meetings, systems, procedures, policies, decisions, etc.)

"When things aren't clear," Dan said, stepping away from the board, "when there's a lack of clarity in the workplace, it only leads to unnecessary and avoidable frustration, confusion, and even resentment. It's hard to have a team work together as effectively as they ought to without clarity around these things." He pointed again to the board where he had written the big-ticket list. "Clarity around these big-ticket items will help you create a healthy culture and become a great boss."

Marty scanned the list while thinking about how unclear many of the things Dan had written on the board as big-ticket items, not to mention the building blocks, had been to him at different centers he had worked at in the past. The more he thought about it, the more he realized there was often confusion around most of them.

Marty also reflected on the lack of cohesion and misalignment that often existed among many of the leadership teams he had been a part of at Wiser Care. He had questioned at times why the CEOs weren't doing more to align the teams. Though he didn't recognize it at the time, he could now see that clarity around the items listed on the board could have resolved most of their problems.

"Let me ask you something," Dan said. "How clear has your role and responsibilities always been during your career? Did you ever feel here at Wiser Care like you did when you were watching the Super Bowl?"

Marty thought for a second before he recalled a situation with the second boss he'd had at Wiser Care, whom he'd gotten along with quite well, all things considered. However, what had frustrated Marty the most about him had been that many important responsibilities had fallen through the cracks. It was as if he wasn't willing to assign people certain tasks for fear they would reject him. As a result, a lot of important things had been left undone, and this had caused problems.

This uncertainty in responsibilities had led people to silently blame others when things didn't get done. A lot of assumptions were made among the different leaders, and results had suffered.

Soon, just when it felt to Marty that trust within the leadership team was at an all-time low, it finally had come to a head. Marty had been the director of the business office at the time, and he'd finally had it and had blown up one day about the nursing staff failing to put all the patient information into the electronic medical record when they were admitted to the center. This significantly slowed down his team's ability to bill and collect money. The VP of nursing had fired back that the nurses were already overloaded with work and that, during an admission, they didn't have time to put in patients' financial information. Her opinion was that Marty's team could easily handle that portion themselves. There were varying opinions within the leadership team on who ultimately held respon-sibility for this task before Marty informed everyone that his department would take on this task for each new admission. Though there was some relief the issue had been settled, the damage had been done.

In retrospect, Marty knew his approach to dealing with his frustration at the time was wrong, but it was an issue that needed to get resolved if he hoped to reach his department's goals, which he did. Unfortunately, not all misunderstandings like this got resolved. Though Marty, for the most part, learned to stay above the fray after this incident, finger-pointing and blaming others were standard operating procedures at this center as confusion around roles and responsibilities persisted. To say this lack of clarity hurt the results at the center was an understatement in Marty's mind.

"Yes. I guess I can think of some instances when things were not made clear to me, but that didn't stop me from working hard or trying to do a good job," Marty replied unconvincingly.

"OK, I bet that's true, but how much better would you have felt if clarity had existed? And how much more do you think you could have contributed as a result of this clarity?" Dan asked.

Again, there was no doubt in Marty's mind his results would have been better, not to mention his relationships with his coworkers. Marty had wasted a lot of time feeling frustrated and angry toward those he worked with at that center, and he knew most others had similar feelings as well. Marty had to concur that Dan had a point.

"OK, it definitely would have been better," Marty said.

"As you may have experienced in the past, important things can often slip through the cracks, and a lot of redundancy and duplicate work can happen when roles and responsibilities aren't clear. When members of a team aren't clear on who's in charge of what, it opens the doors to a lot of problems—such as finger-pointing, blaming others, and mistrust, to name a few."

Marty had to smile to himself because he knew exactly what Dan was talking about. The memory Dan's questions had provoked reminded him he had experienced it firsthand.

Dan continued. "And the real problem isn't that something fell through the cracks. That's more of the symptom of the actual problem, as I see it. The real problem is it wasn't made completely clear who was responsible to take ownership of it."

Marty thought about Dan's last point, and he could understand how it was accurate. Many of the issues the team faced with his second boss could have been resolved with more clarity.

Dan interrupted Marty's thoughts. "The next on the list below, 'roles and responsibilities,' is the evaluation process, including how often you'll have formal reviews and what criteria people will be measured on. When people don't know this, I've found they spend too much time thinking about it, and often discouragement can set in. However, when this is made very clear from the beginning, people often perform as you'd like them to, and they'll know if they're doing a good job or not. They'll also know when they will be receiving formal, direct feedback.

"Next is your 'standards and expectations,' which must also be made very clear," Dan said, pointing to the next item on his list with the marker. "This includes standards and expectations for the group as well as for each individual. The standards set a minimum expectation of performance, meaning if we can't reach this mark, then we are in real big trouble. Expectations are things you expect the person to do, whether it's daily, weekly, monthly, and so on. Clear standards and expectations also inform the team what is and isn't acceptable.

"It's also important you make goals extremely clear." Dan moved the marker down the list. "Like performance standards and expectations, this should include team goals as well as individual goals. Goals should be what the team is stretching and truly striving for. They should be designed to push the team to better performance. And this includes clarity around both short- and long-term goals. If your people aren't clear on what the performance standards are as well as the goals you're trying to achieve, it will be unlikely they'll live up to them or ever succeed at achieving them."

Marty nodded. This seemed right to him.

"The next on my big-ticket list," Dan continued, "is 'results.' People like to know where they stand and how they are doing. They want to be a part of a winning team, and they want to know where they can contribute. When results aren't clear,

44

people begin to lose interest, or they begin to guess and make assumptions. When this happens, people may unintentionally believe the team is doing great when it's not or that they're on a sinking ship when just the opposite is true. When results are very clear in each person's mind on your team, it allows them to better focus on the things that matter most."

Dan now put the marker down and stood away from the board, saying, "The final item on my list is what I call 'the why.' Much like the mission and vision provide purpose, helping people understand and then reminding them why you have certain meetings, live by certain practices, follow certain policies, or implement certain systems is so important to helping them see their value. Just like with the mission, when people understand why you do what you do, it's a lot easier to support it and embrace it. People can even get really excited about a meeting, for example, when the purpose of that meeting is well defined and made clear."

Marty raised his eyebrow as he heard this. He knew the number of people who openly complained about all the meetings they had to attend, and it seemed like an ongoing struggle to help people embrace the necessity of them.

Dan didn't seem to notice Marty's reaction and added, "Without the why, systems, meetings, even policies and procedures can seem like unnecessary nuisances or even feel like a complete waste of time. When this kind of clarity doesn't exist, people will often complain or fight against things that are actually serving them in their work." Marty had to agree and nodded as Dan looked his way again.

Dan now moved back to his chair and sat on the edge of it as if he might stand back up at any moment. He then looked Marty in the eyes and said seriously, "Your people need to know these things; better yet, they *deserve* to know these things. And if they don't know them, you open the door to confusion and misalignment throughout your team. Trust me." Dan looked very intense. "When your people know what is important to you as their boss, they'll try to do those things. When they know what needs to be done in order to have good performance, they'll strive to reach it. When goals and results are clear, people will know what's expected. Clarity brings alignment to your team. And when a team is aligned, it accelerates and fosters high performance. The more clarity you provide around everything, but especially around these building blocks and big-ticket items on the board, the better your results will be."

Scooting back a little in his chair now and appearing to relax some, Dan said, "The more clarity you establish, the better people will feel about where they work and who they work for. They will perform for you, Marty."

Marty's thoughts turned to all the unproductive and divisive communication that seemed so prevalent surrounding many of the items listed on the board. Gossip, rumors, and feelings of uncertainty ran rampant in many of the centers where he had worked. He thought how providing clarity around these items would put an end to, or at least greatly diminish, the behind-the-scenes chatter that seemed to permeate most centers.

Dan added, "The building blocks listed on the board shouldn't change much, so your message on those will always be the same. The big-ticket items, on the other hand, might constantly be adjusting to meet the needs and demands of your business. Again, clarity around both the building blocks and big-ticket items will be incredibly important to your success. Clarity will help you become a great leader."

As this all began to sink in a little, the office phone on the desk rang. Marty instinctively looked at Dan almost as if asking who should answer it. Dan chuckled, pointed at Marty, and said,

"Don't even think about it. You're the boss now, not me. It must be important because I asked Kate and the team to hold your calls, so you better answer it." And with that, Marty picked up his first call in his new office, a call he wouldn't soon forget.

Kate's Concern

"I'm sorry. I really didn't want to interrupt you and Dan," Kate, Marty's executive assistant, whom he had met earlier, said quickly on the other end of the line. To Marty she sounded nervous. "I feel like maybe I made a big mistake."

"What is it?" Marty asked, now becoming nervous himself about what Kate might have done. Thoughts of *This could be my first big test to prove myself* followed by *But I'm not ready yet* flashed through his mind as he wondered anxiously what it could be.

"I told Dr. Simpson that we had rescheduled his patient…"

Marty knew about Dr. Simpson as he'd heard about him in the past. He was an important referral source and customer of the health care center, but at times he could be a pain, often making unreasonable requests and demands. Stories had circulated throughout Wiser Care about how Dan on more than one occasion had skillfully maneuvered through some sticky situations and managed to not only salvage but also strengthen the relationship. Marty was prepared to do whatever it took to win Dr. Simpson over as Dan had. Marty did not know about rescheduling a patient of Dr. Simpson's, but he knew it couldn't be good.

Kate continued. "And then he asked to speak with Dan, at which time I informed him of the changes that were taking place here. I'm really sorry."

Marty was confused. He wasn't sure what, exactly, Kate was telling him, but he could feel perspiration begin to form on his forehead. He worried what Dan might think of all this and what he would do if he were still in charge. Gathering his composure a bit, he said, "Hold on, Kate. Relax for a minute, and let's talk this through. Why did we reschedule Dr. Simpson's patient?"

Kate, now sounding confused herself, replied matter-of-factly. "Because he told us to. He has two more patients coming tomorrow, so he wanted to have all three come on the same day. So I quickly rescheduled the one for today to tomorrow. That's not where I might have messed up." Kate sounded a little more flustered.

"So what's the problem then?" Marty responded a little more shortly then he had intended to. He was irritated, mostly because he didn't understand what he was missing.

"Well…" Kate hesitated, sounding nervous again. "I wasn't sure if I was supposed to tell him about the leadership change or not. It was never made very clear to me how we were informing our doctors and other outside partners of the news. I assumed we had informed Dr. Simpson; in fact, I was pretty sure of it, so when he asked me what Dan was up to and why he couldn't speak to him now, I just responded honestly, and he got upset at me. I hope I didn't mess up by letting him know you were here now as Dan's replacement."

And there it was, Marty thought as he chuckled a little bit to himself and calmed down. Exactly on cue. Almost as if Dan and Kate had planned this out weeks ago, a lesson on clarity and what a lack of it can do. First Kate felt unsure and interrupted Marty, which then made Marty nervous, all because there was a little piece of clarity missing about how the health care center wanted to advise the outside world of the change in leadership. After all, Dan had been *the man* there in that community for two decades, so people were bound to be upset knowing he

49

was gone. Marty imagined the implications a lack of clarity could have on his health care center, especially when it came to things even more important.

"Well, how did it end with Dr. Simpson?" Marty asked calmly.

"He said what he wanted to talk to Dan about really wasn't a big deal and that he would introduce himself to you later and then hung up on me abruptly. I shouldn't have broken the news to him in that way. I'm sorry."

"No, Kate, it's really not a big deal. It really is our fault for not making things very clear to you, the team, and Dr. Simpson for that matter. I'm sure I can smooth things over with him. I'll give him a call right away."

"OK, good. I just wanted to make sure I didn't step out of line is all...with you, I mean...on your first day," Kate said, still sounding somewhat nervous.

Marty understood that most of Kate's nervousness was because she had a new boss and didn't really know him. He also assumed she had liked working for Dan and that the transition was probably scary for most of the team. Marty wanted her and the others to feel as comfortable as they always had with Dan.

"Listen, Kate, it really is our fault, and what you told Dr. Simpson is fine. I'd like you to act and behave just as you did when Dan was in charge. Sound OK? And one more thing." Marty continued before she could answer. "I'd like to chat with you for a few minutes before you leave for the day about something I believe you can really help me with. I have some questions about how some things are done around here, and I'd like to learn from you about them."

"Yes, sir," Kate responded, sounding a little more confident now. "I'll talk to you then."

Marty hung up the phone.

"What was that all about?" Dan asked as Marty leaned back, shaking his head a little bit.

"Are you sure you and Kate didn't talk today...about what you were going to share with me?" Marty asked with a big smile across his face as he pictured Dan coordinating people to interrupt their conversations just at the precise moment to drive home his points.

"No, why?" Dan responded innocently. "Is everything OK?"

"Yes," Marty said, "except I think Kate drilled home your point a little bit about making *everything* clear." He smiled to himself again while exaggerating the word *everything*.

Marty went on to explain what had happened and the initial confusion he felt when Kate reported the problem. Both men had a good laugh, and then Dan said, "It's amazing how a lack of clarity on some seemingly obvious things can cause problems. One thing you must know, Marty, is that in this position, if you want to do a good job, you'll find yourself repeating yourself a lot. And I mean a lot a lot," he said with emphasis.

Marty thought about that when Dan leaned back and said, "I've told Dr. Simpson more than once that I was retiring, and we sent a letter to his office just like we did with all our community partners. Dr. Simpson is always in such a hurry and always has so much on his mind...he just doesn't stop to hear things sometimes." He shook his head. "And that's one reason why working with him can be hard, but we'll talk about him later." Dan had a bit of a sarcastic smile that made Marty feel a little uneasy.

Straightening up in his chair, Dan added, "This actually brings up a great point about clarity."

Marty wasn't sure what Dan was referring to. "Like I mentioned, repeating yourself often is the key to establishing clarity, so get used to it. Especially with Dr. Simpson," Dan said, now smiling in a more genuine way.

Then, more serious, he added, "Once you feel like you've said the same things over and over and over and over again is when you can begin to feel good that you are making some progress, especially around the items on the board. I've heard it takes at least seven times for someone to hear a message before they will even begin to internalize and understand it. Seven!" Dan held up seven fingers and raised his eyebrows for emphasis.

Marty was wondering again about the implications of establishing clarity when Dan continued. "I also obviously missed a big opportunity to be clearer by telling Kate about our communication plan with our external partners and community on the upcoming leadership change. Kate should never have felt like she was unsure of what to say to Dr. Simpson." He looked a little upset. "And though Dr. Simpson and I talked about my departure on more than one occasion, it appears it wasn't enough for it to really sink in. So let this be a reminder to you that people need to hear things at least seven times."

Dan paused for a moment when suddenly his cell phone began to ring. Quickly fetching it out of his pocket and peering down at it in his hand, he said, "It's my wife. Let's take just a minute." Marty nodded, and before he could say anything, Dan put the phone to his ear and said, "Hello, sweetheart."

Marty decided this was a great time to make a quick call himself. He picked up the phone and dialed Dr. Simpson.

Most Important Role

As Dan and Marty returned to the same chairs they'd been sitting in before, Dan said, "Sorry about that, Marty. Normally when I'm in the middle of a conversation with someone, I wouldn't grab that, but today was supposed to be my first day of retirement, so I'm trying to stay on good terms with Mrs. Rosier." He smiled and added, "If I don't, I may be banished to work all the rest of my days." Both men laughed almost in unison.

"No, that's OK," said Marty. "Really. It actually gave me a chance to call Dr. Simpson and clear things up. He's fine, and we'll be meeting tomorrow afternoon after his three patients arrive."

"That's great," Dan said. Marty noticed a look of approval come across Dan's face, which made him feel good about his responsiveness to an important partner and customer.

"Dr. Simpson can be a little difficult at times, but he's a great doctor who pushes those around him to be their best. When you understand that about him, that he has high standards for all those who work in health care, it makes you want to work with him and be better. Once you get to know him, it becomes easy to accept some of his weaknesses because of all his strengths," Dan added.

Marty thought about that as Dan continued. "As you can see with the Dr. Simpson and Kate incident, I'm still not perfect at this. I've had so much I've been trying to wrap up before my final day that I didn't clearly let Kate know about how to respond to people when questioned about the leadership change. This isn't a good excuse, but what I'm trying to say is making things clear is a constant, daily effort for great leaders. There's no finish line with clarity. It must always be at the top of your priority list. When you aren't constantly striving to establish clarity, you'll have Kate and Dr. Simpson–type situations like we had today, only they'll have the potential to cause *a lot* worse consequences." Dan emphasized the words *a lot* while sliding back in his chair and appearing to relax a bit.

"I know I've already said this more than once, but repetition is your key to success with clarity. You may get tired of repeating the same things, but it's so important that you stick with it. Establishing clarity across the health care center is perhaps your most important role here as the leader in charge. I can't think of any other way you could add more value in your new position."

Marty was surprised by how strongly Dan felt about this first *C*. He honestly had never really considered how important clarity was; nor had he ever thought about it much in his prior leadership roles. Sure, he had tried to be clear about important things, but he never consciously had it as a priority. He could understand how clarity made leaders more effective and easier to work for, but was it really his *most* important role?

Dan stood now and walked behind the chair he'd been sitting in, placing his hands on the back of it to support his weight. "If you'll allow me to, Marty, I'd like to share a story from earlier in my management career here at Wiser Care."

"Sure," Marty said sincerely. "Please share."

"I was given a temporary assignment to lead a small health care center that was struggling. My assignment was to keep it together for two months while also trying to clean up some things before the new permanent CEO arrived. I knew I would be evaluated on my performance and that the company wanted to see how I'd do leading a center, even if it was just for a short time."

Marty was familiar with this practice as many times aspiring leaders at Wiser Care would be pulled out of their normal positions of responsibility to fill in temporarily where there was a leadership vacancy.

"My very first day at work there, I gathered the entire leadership team together and informed them I wanted a daily written report from each of them on their progress toward improving their specific areas of responsibility. I explained how I expected communication to be at an all-time high and that I felt it was necessary for me to have a good general idea of where each department stood, given the challenges the operation was facing. I explained that these reports should include not only their progress but also any setbacks they were having that I could help them with. I assured them I'd read them over each day. I even showed them a good example of the kind of report I was expecting and provided some questions they could answer for me in their written reports. Finally, I let them know it was unacceptable not to hand in a daily report. I was sure I had made myself really clear and felt everyone knew exactly what was required."

Dan moved back in front of his chair and sat, looking down at the ground and shaking his head a little. "I felt so confident and sure that everyone knew exactly where I stood and what I wanted from them."

Dan paused for a moment before looking up and continuing. "Nearly all the department heads gave me exactly what I was looking for without any problems with the exception of one person. What surprised me about this person was he frequently stopped in to tell me what he was up to, but I had clearly stated I wanted reports on paper. After a few days, his verbal updates began to really get on my nerves, but something surprised me. I noticed this individual was staying later than others and seemed to be working really hard to do a good job; however, there were still no written reports. I began to mention things casually and drop hints in our conversations and meetings but still nothing. The longer this went on, the more irritated I became, and it began to show. I became very short with him whenever he came to give me a verbal update."

Dan stopped, and Marty could see he was reflecting back to the moment. "I hate to admit it now, but at the time, the fact that he wasn't giving me written reports bothered me so much that I began to try to avoid him altogether. My thought was if he couldn't give me a verbal report, maybe it would force him to give me a written report, which is what I really wanted from him."

Dan paused, frowned, furrowed his brow, and said, "Now that I think about it, for some reason, Marty, back in those days, I felt I had to have everything on paper. I suppose because it gave me something tangible that I could have to prove how hard we were all working if I was ever questioned. This probably sounds pretty strange to you. My, how things have changed." Dan shook his head.

Marty nodded and smiled but decided not to interrupt.

"You must think by now I'm both really old and a terrible leader." Dan smiled, relaxing a bit.

Marty felt it might be a good idea to lighten the mood a little and couldn't resist. "No doubt you are an ancient person, Dan, but I'm still evaluating your leadership abilities," he said with a big smile, and Dan laughed out loud.

"Well, I'm glad we got that out on the table," Dan said, still chuckling.

Marty added, "I'm only joking. You know that, right?" He was a little worried he might have gone too far.

Dan looked at Marty a little skeptically as if he wasn't sure if he could trust him, and they both laughed again. Marty enjoyed that Dan was teasing him back.

"Anyway," Dan continued, beginning to sound more serious again, "despite my hints to this person, I still had nothing from him in terms of a written report. This went on for a little while longer until finally, I'd had it with this department head. After some incident that upset me, I came to the decision I needed to confront this leader. So I grabbed several reports that the others had handed in and headed straight for his work area. I was prepared to show him how far behind he was in his reporting and demand that he get me something right away."

Dan blew out some air as he sat back in his chair. "Boy, was I mistaken. I confronted this leader in front of others, practically throwing a handful of reports in his face. Then it dawned on me. I'm not sure why it happened right at that moment, but it did. I remembered this person hadn't been in the initial meeting where I had thoroughly explained the importance of reporting to all the department heads. What made things worse for me was the reason he hadn't been at the meeting was because he willingly covered for a nurse that day who wasn't able to make it to work. So he not only did his own work that day but also the work of others. I felt incredibly embarrassed as this realization popped into my head, but rather than say anything, I stormed off, feeling ashamed by what I had just done."

"Wow," Marty said softly, a little surprised. He could tell how bad Dan felt, so he added, "But that's a mistake any of us could make. I mean, it was innocent. We all make mistakes. And he probably should have asked what he had missed in that meeting."

"This may be true, but I had let this thing eat at me. The amount of energy it drained, the stress it caused, and how it distracted me from what I should have been focused on could have all been avoided with a little more clarity. If I had just reiterated my expectations of the written report and why it was important a few more times, making sure my expectations and performance standards were clear to everyone, I could have avoided the whole fiasco."

Marty could see Dan's point, but he still felt Dan was maybe being too hard on himself.

"And the thing is, Marty, even if this department head had been in that meeting, rarely do people get the message the first time we tell them. Remember the seven-times rule?"

Marty thought about that for a moment as Dan went on. "Making sure your expectations are clear by repeating them often is so important. I learned from this experience how important clarity is, and I wish I could say I've been perfect ever since. But the reality is there have been many similar instances where I failed to use clarity to my advantage. Even now I'm always working at it." Dan still looked a little dejected after reflecting on how he'd treated this department head long ago.

Marty wanted to say something that would help Dan feel better, but he wasn't sure what.

"In fact, the biggest mistake leaders make with clarity is believing they have been clear when the reality is, they haven't been. It's awful feeling like everyone should know what you want, and then you get upset about it only to find out people had no idea. That you hadn't really taken the time to be clear."

Dan paused for a moment before adding, "Clarity is a powerful leadership tool, and the funny thing is that it is not only incredibly effective but also free. It doesn't cost you anything. And *all* leaders can use it if they decide to, regardless of their expertise or experience," Dan said, looking at Marty. Marty nodded to show he agreed.

Marty felt he was really beginning to understand why clarity was the first *C* and the foundation of Dan's model for leadership success. He was grateful Dan had shared such a personal story with him, although it was still hard for him to imagine Dan behaving the way he had depicted in his story. Marty had what he felt was an important question.

Important Question

"So how do I make sure things are clear?" Marty asked genuinely.

"I thought you'd never ask," Dan responded with a little smile.

"You can never overcommunicate with your people." Dan looked closely at Marty as if double-checking to make sure he was listening. "Again, let me repeat it to you. I believe as a leader you can never overcommunicate. It's just impossible. In order to establish a high level of clarity, you need to become a broken record and repeat yourself often. Especially around the building blocks and the big-ticket items as we discussed. Let me reiterate that I mean over and over and over again," Dan said, rolling his right arm in a circular motion in front of him. Marty had to chuckle at Dan's enthusiasm. "Not only do you need to discuss these things repeatedly, but also you need to find ways to reinforce them."

Dan paused for a moment as if he were about to say something important. Marty turned his head slightly to listen. "One of the best ways to do that is by making them an important part of your people systems."

Marty raised one of his eyebrows, not exactly sure he understood what Dan had just said. Dan seemed to know it was coming and quickly added, "People systems are any of your processes that deal with people, such as your interviewing process, your onboarding process, new employee orientation, rewards and recognition systems, compensation and incentives, meetings, employee evaluation processes, and even disciplinary and termination processes. All of these people systems should reinforce the building blocks. The building blocks should be the focal point of each."

Marty made a note to ask Kate and his human resources director about this.

"You can also reinforce them in all forms of communication, like emails, memos, newsletters, bulletin boards, even T-shirts and gifts. Whatever it is you're doing, find ways to clarify your team's primary purpose or mission, where you are headed or your vision, and the behavioral expectations you stand for or your values. That's how you do it. It can be simple," Dan said with a grin.

"Simple, huh?" Marty said sarcastically. Though it wasn't hard to understand, the idea of constantly communicating and creating clarity did seem a little daunting. It did make sense, though, and Marty began to wonder why more leaders didn't focus on it.

"Let me share just a quick example of what I mean. A few years ago, we wanted people who applied to our health care center to know what matters most to us and make it very clear why we come to work every day. Too many new team members were not getting up to speed fast enough, and they often didn't really realize what they were getting themselves into when joining us." Dan smiled. "So we created an additional page to our formal application where we listed our mission statement and asked how the applicant would help us live our mission every day."

Marty thought that sounded like a great way to establish clarity around the mission. Dan added, "We also took it a step further. We then added our core values to the form and asked the applicant to tell us how they had lived our core values in their lives." He paused for moment before adding, "This simple additional page to our application brought a lot of clarity to those who were applying. It informed them from the beginning what mattered most to us here at our center. After all," Dan said, shrugging, "they had to write a short essay on our mission and values just to apply. We then really hammered the point home by asking them several questions during the interview process about their responses on this particular page of the application. In fact, we don't interview anyone for any position until they have completely filled out this page of our application. It's the first page all interviewers at our center turn to."

Marty leaned back, taking in this simple process and seeing how it would help create clarity around some of the building blocks.

Dan went on. "Because of our desire to improve clarity, people who were just being introduced to our organization quickly understood what we stand for and what we are all about. This tweak to our application then reinforced clarity to everyone involved in the interview process as well."

Marty was impressed by how simple this example was and by how effective he imagined it was at establishing clarity around the most important things. He could understand how making this change provided more clarity throughout the organization as each new employee who started would already have a good idea of what the mission and values of the center are.

Dan continued. "Clarity stimulates trust, which is key to your ability to lead effectively. Clarity also sets the foundation for your success as a leader. In fact, clarity just might be the most important *C* in the model because it establishes the basis for the rest of your culture to be built on. This is why it is at the base of our pyramid over there." Dan turned his head and pointed to what he had written on the whiteboard. "Clarity is the foundation of a strong and healthy culture—it's the foundation that is set by the most effective leaders."

Marty nodded, soaking up the information and knowledge Dan was sharing.

"So constantly finding ways to create clarity will make you a better leader than most other bosses out there because too many don't pay that much attention to it or realize the impact it has." Dan paused as if he wanted that to soak in for a moment. "Though this is only the base of our model, clarity alone can go a long way in helping your health care center thrive and flourish."

"But why stop there, right?" Dan smiled. "Clarity in conjunction with the other three *C*'s will help you have truly great results and do it in a way that's lasting and meaningful."

Marty considered what the other three *C*'s might be. Dan said, "Unfortunately, over the years, it has been my experience that people in authority often aren't very good at creating clarity. Sometimes it may be due to a lack of skill; other times it might be a lack of understanding of how important it is. On rare occasions it may be purposeful, such as a boss withholding or denying clarity because it somehow makes them feel more powerful, important, or in control. Most often, however, leaders believe they're being clear when they're not. This has been my biggest struggle with clarity, and I'm sure it will be yours. You must remember the seven-times rule, Marty. Remember that just because it's clear in your mind doesn't mean it's clear for others. And just because you've said something once or twice doesn't mean anyone has understood it, internalized it, or retained it. Regardless of the reason, you need to avoid the lack-of-clarity trap that happens to way too many leaders and organizations out there. When things are left unclear, it can undermine your other efforts to be an awesome boss."

Marty thought he now knew all about what Dan was describing as it seemed many of the leaders he had worked for had struggled to make the most important things clear. Marty began to worry that he may have even been one of them himself. He certainly knew he wasn't always clear about all the items Dan had listed on the board with the teams and departments he had led in the past. Marty committed to being more open and transparent with those he led and wanted to provide as much clarity as possible to his new team.

Lack of Clarity

"I know I've already talked a lot," Dan said. "But I think it would be wise to tell you another personal story that illustrates the importance of clarity." Marty was curious where Dan would go next and leaned forward in his chair.

"When I first became a COO at Wiser Care many years ago, it was at a large health care center. I was grateful for the opportunity, and things were going well—at least, I thought they were going well. That is, until my director of admissions told me she was quitting."

Marty's interest was piqued as he looked over at Dan, who was shifting in his chair as if trying to get comfortable again. He then said, "You need to understand, Marty, that this director of admissions was amazing. I felt she was a big reason for the center's success. Our center had more patient admissions in a month than many other centers did in a quarter. Needless to say, the admissions director's role was critical at that center." Dan paused for a moment before adding, "I felt, as well as most of the other leaders in the center, that we had one of the best admissions directors out there, but now, after a few months under my watch, she was leaving. As you can imagine, I was panicking."

Marty knew how stressful it was when good people left. Replacing department heads was never easy, and to lose one who was really good, well, that always set the operation back. It could take months for a new department head to get up to speed, and then you never knew for sure how they'd perform. Keeping proven leaders who were successful was so important to any center.

"So I did what every good leader would do in my situation. I begged her to stay," Dan said with a smile. Marty guessed he was only partially joking. "I asked her why she was leaving and was completely shocked by what she told me."

Marty waited in anticipation, wondering what she might have said.

"She said she wasn't sure why, but she wasn't happy at work anymore. She'd been doing the job for a while at that center and felt she was successful at it, but she shared she actually wasn't sure if her performance was good enough for me." Dan paused as if to let that sink in before adding, "Now imagine how my jaw hit the floor upon hearing this. I assumed it was obvious she was doing amazing work, but it wasn't clear to her."

Marty was a little surprised.

"And she didn't stop there. She also reported she didn't feel what she was doing was making much of a difference. She reported to me that she dreaded Monday mornings and didn't want to feel that way any longer."

At that moment Marty felt he could somewhat relate to this department head's feelings, having experienced some of them at different times in the past while working at Wiser Care. Of course, he certainly wasn't about to let Dan know this.

"She then said for these reasons she felt she needed to leave, to find someplace where she could really make a difference, meet expectations, and add value. Yet she was doing wonderful things for us." Dan looked up with a concerned look on his face.

"Wow..." Marty finally said, quietly wondering what happened next.

"I know," Dan said. "I couldn't believe what I was hearing. I nearly fell out of my chair during our conversation. This was one of my best department heads, and she thought she wasn't adding much value or doing a great job!"

"So what did you do?" Marty asked.

Dan sat back and looked as if he was thinking for a moment. "First, I apologized. I told her I was sorry for not communicating with her more. I promised her that I would improve. Next, I explained to her how important she was to the team and how she was helping us live our mission and reach our vision. I told her that she was playing a critical role in the success of the center. Finally, I showed her how our admissions department's performance compared to other sister centers in the organization and how she was leading the way in many of the important metrics. I made certain she knew she was doing a fantastic job and contributing to the success at the center. I decided to take it a step further and showed her the center's performance in the past prior to her arrival and compared it to the performance since her arrival. It was impressive to see her impact on the results within her department."

Marty was impressed by what Dan had done. Dan added, "I tried to do all I could to help her understand how the work she was doing was really making a huge difference in the lives of so many."

Marty thought about this for another moment and decided Dan was pretty smart in how he had handled the tough situation. What Marty really wanted to know now was if it had worked. *Did she stay with the company?* Before he could ask, Dan went on.

"Thankfully, by divine intervention, I'm sure, what I had done made a big difference to her. I could see her eyes light up when she clearly saw how she was performing and how she was impacting our outcomes. We agreed to meet monthly to review the results of our admissions department and compare them to our sister health care centers. We also set clear goals that would help her improve the already-impressive numbers she had in the department, and we tracked performance closely. And though I didn't openly tell her this, I made a conscious effort to remind her often how her job was directly important to our mission and vision for our center. I made sure she knew her work mattered. Thankfully, all this seemed to change things for her, and she stayed."

Marty sat back, still impressed by what Dan had done and feeling relieved about how things had turned out. "Pretty nifty maneuvering there," Marty finally said, trying to give Dan a hard time, adding, "Sounds like your quick thinking really paid off."

"It did pay off, but I hope you aren't missing the point here. It should have never gotten to that point. The complete lack of clarity that existed among those I was supposed to be leading was beyond troublesome. Without that conversation, I'm sure we would have lost her and probably others. I almost lost one of my best leaders because of a lack of clarity."

Marty nodded slowly now as he fully realized how clarity, or the lack thereof, had caused a significant problem. Dan continued. "That experience opened my eyes to how important it is to provide clarity. Too often leaders think things are clear when they're not. I thought this department head of mine knew she was doing amazing work, but looking back, I realized I'd rarely mentioned it to her, so how would she have known? Most of those things on the list over there"—Dan pointed to the board—"were not clear."

Though Dan had told Marty he hadn't always strived to implement the four C's, Marty still felt surprised hearing about a time when Dan didn't provide good clarity to his team. This actually made him feel a little better about himself and his performance as a leader over the years. Though he hadn't thought about clarity the way Dan had helped him think about it today, Marty did believe he was a leader who did better at it than others. Now, having it laid out by Dan and feeling he was finally grasping its importance, Marty knew this knowledge would help him improve.

Dan went on. "When there's a lack of clarity, your people can easily feel they're stuck in a rut or like their jobs don't have significance or that they aren't really accomplishing or contributing to anything great."

Marty was still considering all Dan was sharing when he added, "Without clarity, often people won't feel successful. In fact, they may not know where they stand at all, and that is a bad feeling."

Marty waited a few seconds to make sure Dan had finished before saying, "I agree that this story is a good illustration of how important the first C can be. Thank-you for sharing it with me."

"My pleasure," Dan replied, quickly adding, "Can I share one more simple example of what we're doing here in our health care center to improve clarity?"

"Please do share," Marty replied, genuinely excited to hear more.

"About fifteen years ago, we really started having some problems. Though my first four years here proved successful, year five started out slow and then got worse. We began to really struggle, so much so that the corporate office offered to send in some extra help to assist us in getting back on track. I didn't want that, and I knew our team could figure it out. We had some new department heads in key positions, and things just weren't clicking as they should have been.

"With time, it became very apparent that my team wasn't communicating well, and too many leaders began making decisions in isolation that affected others. There were just a lot of assumptions being made. I knew my team was frustrated with one another, and I was extremely frustrated because my efforts to be clear weren't working well enough." Dan moved uncomfortably in his chair. "I'm actually still bothered as I think about our substantial drop in performance the first half of that year—it just never should have happened." He looked a little upset and shook his head slowly.

Marty was very intrigued to hear more, but he also couldn't resist the temptation to have some fun with Dan. "You're right; maybe you aren't such a great leader after all." Marty tried to sound as serious as possible, but he couldn't keep a straight face when Dan looked up quickly and seemed surprised.

"Sorry. I couldn't resist," Marty said, laughing now. "Please go on." Marty wondered if he should have interrupted Dan. He really was curious to know what happened next and hoped Dan didn't take his jest to mean something different.

Dan hesitated, then chuckled, relaxing a bit as if he finally fully realized Marty was having some fun with him again. "It's a good thing I'm retiring. I'm not sure I could keep up with you young troublemakers these days."

"Sorry about that; I really do want to know what happened next. I shouldn't have interrupted."

Dan waved his hand as if it was no big deal. "Let's see, where was I? Oh yes. Though I responded slower to our communication problem than I should have, I gathered with my core team of leaders here at the center, and we decided together to implement a short meeting at the beginning of each day with our entire leadership team.

"Now, you know how people feel about additional meetings, so we knew this wouldn't be a popular idea. But we reasoned if we were focused and concise in this meeting, it would take us only about ten minutes each day. We also believed it could really help us improve clarity."

Marty knew how most leaders responded to the idea of extra meetings, and he was sure Dan had received pushback on this potential solution to their problem. Though he wasn't sure how he felt about holding a daily morning meeting, he was intrigued to hear more.

"Once we introduced the idea, there was some resistance and plenty of good reasons why it didn't seem sensible. However, I could also detect that our team knew we probably needed it, so we started having the meetings." Dan paused for a minute. "One of my directors at the time loved football, and he coined these meetings our 'Daily Morning Huddle,' and the name stuck. In fact, the analogy grew, and we soon were huddling each day to discuss our 'play for that day,' as we still like to call it."

Marty smiled and waited for Dan to continue.

Dan went on, expanding on the football comparison. "Just think about what would happen in a football game if no one knew what the next play was. Imagine if everyone had to guess which play to run. Think about the confusion and frustration that would set in if the running back assumed it was going to be a run play, but the quarterback assumed it was a pass play. Or if the lineman blocked for a short screen pass instead of a long bomb. Is there any way that football team would be successful?"

"I highly doubt it," Marty replied. He smiled at the thought of it.

"Such was the status of my team. I believe we were all mostly well intentioned, but we were running different plays each day. Marketing thought it was a long bomb, while nursing thought it was a simple run play. So we determined we needed morning huddles to get everyone on the same page—we all needed to know the play."

Dan paused, looking at Marty as if he thought Marty was going to say something. Marty didn't have anything to add at this point, so he sat forward, quietly waiting, and Dan continued. "Like a huddle in a football game, this morning huddle is quick yet effective. It typically lasts ten to fifteen minutes at most, yet it allows our leadership team to share quickly what each is up to and to get on the same page. Simple things that normally take multiple emails and cross communication get ironed out in less than a minute." Dan sat back in his chair again. "Best of all, it gives me a chance to share a unifying message with my entire leadership team each day. I can focus our efforts on our highest priorities. This quick daily meeting or huddle helped us reestablish tremendous clarity among our team. Before long, we were running the same play each day, and our results turned around."

Again, Marty was impressed with the simplicity yet effectiveness of what Dan was doing at the center to create clarity. Marty wanted to learn so much more.

"This daily huddle did more for us than we ever imagined it would. Though we saw it as a simple way to improve communication, it also brought us closer together as a team and has even helped us with some of the other C's in the model. I can't imagine life at this point without this daily morning huddle."

"I think I'm beginning to understand the importance of clarity," Marty stated. He had a million thoughts running through his head, but the prevailing one was that he was sure clarity was going to be critical to his success as a CEO.

Then a reassuring but also worrisome thought came to his mind. *This is only the first one! And I have to do three more!* Marty began to wonder what the other three C's could be and how difficult they'd be to implement.

Looking at the clock on the wall behind Dan, Marty realized it was past noon. For a split second, he considered trying to persuade Dan to stay longer to explain the rest of the C's, but then he thought better of it. He couldn't ask Dan to do such a thing when he was supposed to be enjoying retirement. Instead, Marty asked, "Can you give me any other examples of what you've done to help with clarity before you go?" He hoped to learn just a little bit more.

Dan smiled. "I could probably talk your ear off all week about clarity if you let me, but trust me, you don't want that right now. Just remember that people like to be in the know; they like to see clearly. It helps them feel important, and it brings alignment to your team. The more you communicate and provide clarity for your team, the better. You should strive to make everything as clear as you possibly can. Never forget that repetition is the key to clarity."

As the two leaders sat in silence for a moment, Marty reflected on all Dan had shared with him that morning. Like a ton of bricks, it finally hit Marty that Dan really had learned the importance of each C through his many experiences. The thought came into his mind that over the next four days, he would be learning what it took Dan an entire career to understand. Marty felt incredibly grateful Dan was sharing the knowledge he had acquired from his many years of service as a leader.

Marty leaned back in his chair, sensing Dan was about to wrap up things for the day.

Departure

Dan sighed a little bit and then leaned back in his chair. "Now, I know this is your first day on the job, and you have a lot to do today, but let me share just one more thing with you on clarity because I still feel I haven't been *clear* enough." A quick smile came across Dan's face again as he slowed down to emphasize the word *clear* just as Marty had done earlier in the day.

Marty enjoyed it and smiled genuinely as Dan continued. "You know you're becoming clear enough only when your team members start finishing your sentences. Until then, keep communicating and clarifying. There's nothing more enjoyable for me than when one of my staff members interrupts me and says, 'I know, I know...' and they finish my sentence for me. Then and only then do you know you're making good progress with the first *C*."

Marty had to laugh to himself, imagining people interrupting Dan and completing his sentences for him. He could tell Dan was serious, and he could even imagine Dan repeating himself over and over again to his team. Marty wondered if his people ever got annoyed by it. Though he wasn't sure, he could tell by walking around the health care center that the people who worked there loved and respected Dan.

"Well, it's getting late now, and I've taken up your entire morning, so I believe I'll head home to try and enjoy my first afternoon of retirement while you get some work done around here. Honestly, Marty, if we stopped here and you applied just the first *C*, the base of the model, it would make you a much better leader—better than most others out there who don't understand the importance of it or pay that much attention to it."

As Marty considered that thought, Dan added, "But let's not stop here. Let's make sure you have all four *C*'s that will help you become an amazing leader." Dan smiled and stood to leave. "I look forward to our time together tomorrow."

"I can't thank you enough for your time today," Marty replied with sincerity. The two stood and shook hands. "I look forward to learning the other three *C*'s soon." And he meant it.

As Dan walked toward the door of the office, Marty couldn't help but feel a sense of respect for this man. Though he hadn't known Dan more than a few hours, he already felt an unexpected level of admiration for him. He knew what Dan had shared with him today was invaluable. Now he just needed to follow through with it and do it!

***

After meeting with Dan all morning, Marty quickly was reintroduced to the reality and demands of running a health care center. Rushing to different meetings, working through multiple unexpected problems, and getting to know more staff filled the rest of Marty's very busy day. He also met with Kate as promised, and she shared her insights on clarity with him.

Though it was now late into the evening and he was feeling pretty overwhelmed by all that needed to be done, Marty felt good about where he was working and what he was doing. He admitted to his wife that night that he sincerely enjoyed his first day at his new center more than he ever expected he would.

What he didn't share with her was what kept coming back to him throughout the day: the conversation he and Dan had had that morning. With his mind fixated on clarity, Marty noticed a few things that were happening at the health care center that helped promote clarity among the team. He also observed that what they were doing to establish clarity was working. Like no other group of employees he had worked with before, everyone seemed aligned and interested in doing a good job. Though there were always improvements that could be made in any health care center, Marty was grateful to be at a center that seemed to be functioning extremely well.

Part Two

Consistency

The Second *C*

It was a bright, beautiful early fall morning, and Marty arrived at the office with an extra hop in his step. Though he hadn't slept much as he'd spent most of the night thinking about his center and what Dan had taught him, he still felt energized as the morning sun shone through his window and onto the office floor near his desk. One thought Marty had while lying awake in the middle of the night was that his team might be able to teach him more about clarity and the other three *C*'s. Kate, after all, had given him some good insight, and he was sure others could as well. Marty made a note of it.

As he wrote the note down, feelings of inadequacy washed over him momentarily as he realized his team knew more about the four *C*'s model than he did. Marty quickly pushed those feelings aside, concluding that not only could he learn a lot from his new team, but also he could teach them a few things. After all, he reasoned, he had been very successful during his career at Wiser Care to this point, and he knew he had a lot to offer, even if the four *C*'s were something new to him.

Taking a big bite out of his breakfast bagel, he sat down at his desk. Suddenly, there was a knock at the door.

"Come on in," Marty hollered across the room with his mouth still full and crumbs spraying everywhere. *Oh man, am I a slob!* he thought to himself as he quickly grabbed a tissue from the Kleenex box on his desk and began to wipe himself off.

Dan opened the door, saying, "OK, that was strange. After you spend so much time in a place, you get used to doing things a certain way. Knocking on this door is something I'm not used to doing." He paused, looking down and shaking his head slightly as if considering the reality of not holding the key to the office anymore. "To be honest, I almost barged right in like I always used to, but something told me I should be a little more respectful and knock. It was hard for me, but I did it. All good things must come to an end," he almost mumbled to himself.

Marty was still examining his shirt for crumbs. Sensing Dan was now looking at him, Marty looked up, and Dan flashed him a big smile. "And by the look of things, I guess I made the right decision to knock first," he said as Marty wiped his hands and threw the tissue in the trash. Quickly swallowing the remaining food in his mouth, Marty grinned back. Dan walked forward, offering his hand, and Marty stood to shake it.

"Please, Dan, this will always be your office," Marty offered. "You don't ever have to knock. I mean it." Marty was serious. After yesterday, he was excited to spend as much time as possible with Dan. In his mind, Dan could do whatever he'd like at this health care center. He had built something special here and had certainly earned it.

Dan stuck his index finger up, wagged it back and forth, and said, "I believe I do need to knock because the last thing I want to happen is to be caught up in the middle of another weekly budget meeting. In fact, I think I'd better lay low around here. There do have to be some perks to retiring, you know." Dan was now smiling and ducking his head as if he were attempting to avoid being seen. Marty laughed at Dan's antics and sat back down. His shoulders relaxed, and he leaned back in his chair and put his hands behind his head. He was feeling more comfortable with Dan and truly enjoyed his presence at the center.

Dan sat down in the same chair as yesterday, across from Marty's desk. Sitting up on the edge of his seat and looking more serious, he said, "Well, should I let you enjoy your breakfast first before we get started?"

"Yes, of course," Marty replied, quickly clarifying. "I mean, of course, let's get started. No reason to waste any of our precious time." Marty meant it. He pushed the bagel off his desk directly into the trash can beside it.

"Well, OK, then," Dan said, raising his eyebrows. "You know, I'm technically retired, and you know what they say retired people have a lot of, don't you?" With a slight smile coming back to the corners of his mouth, he quickly went on. "Time! I'm sure relaxing for a minute while you finished your breakfast wouldn't have slowed us down too much, but I guess it's too late for that now." Dan grinned and looked down at the half-eaten bagel now resting at the bottom of the trash can.

"Really," Marty replied, waving a hand toward the trash, "it wasn't that enjoyable, and after being up all night thinking about how I can provide more clarity in my new role, I'm very eager to learn the next C."

Dan raised his eyebrows again and nodded slightly. Marty noticed what seemed to him to be a look of approval and moved from the chair behind his desk to the chair next to Dan.

"I see you mean business, so let's get going." Dan sat back slightly in his chair, still looking pleased. "I must warn you, however, that the second C I'm about to explain is perhaps the most challenging to establish because it requires a tremendous amount of discipline and commitment on your part. As a leader, you have to make a conscious daily effort, Marty—an effort that many bosses aren't willing to make, an effort that usually doesn't come naturally to many of us. But if you want to be an effective leader and have success, your results after applying this C will convince you that the effort is well worth it."

Marty moved to the edge of his seat. He was ready to learn the second *C*.

"The next *C*, Marty, is hard for all of us. As human beings, many of us tend to fail miserably at it; however, the most successful in life find a way to achieve some level of it."

Marty began to shake the pen in his hand a bit, wondering if Dan was purposely leaving him in suspense. Finally, Dan rather abruptly said, "The next *C* is 'consistency.'"

Marty stopped shaking the pen and wrote the word down on his notepad. "OK," he said waiting for an explanation while also thinking, *Nope, this isn't a C word I would have ever guessed.*

"Do you mind?" Dan motioned to the whiteboard.

"Be my guest," Marty replied, extending his arm toward it. Dan walked over and added another layer of the pyramid to the board. This is what it looked like:

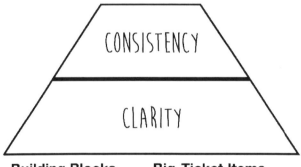

Building Blocks
- Mission
- Vision
- Values

Big-Ticket Items
- Roles & Responsibilities
- Evaluation Process
- Standards & Expectations
- Goals
- Results
- "The Why" (for meetings, systems, procedures, policies, decisions, etc.)

Dan now continued with what Marty was beginning to recognize as his serious tone of voice. "Things in this world can be pretty unpredictable. Heck, just take a look at the latest news feed."

Marty thought about the truthfulness of that.

"Most of us strive to find some level of stability in our lives. Consistency at work brings a level of predictability we all crave."

Marty instantly thought about all the many changes there had been during his time at Wiser Care. How things were done when he started nine years ago was very different from how they operated now. The technology they used, how they were reimbursed, the way they interacted with customers, and even the services and care they now offered were all different. It didn't seem Wiser Care had been very consistent in Marty's mind at that moment. Was Dan suggesting Wiser Care should have continued to do things the way it had always done them and not change at all? That didn't seem right.

Marty knew he must be missing something. He turned his attention back to Dan, who was saying, "And consistency from you, in particular, will bring your team stability and the peace of mind they need to function at their best."

Dan paused for a moment, peering at Marty as if to make sure he'd heard him. Marty nodded slightly to show he was listening, and Dan continued. "Consistency also brings about results. In fact, a lot of leaders who fail, fail because they aren't consistent, especially with the small things." Dan now paused again as if waiting for Marty to say something.

Marty only wanted to hear more at this point, so he said, "OK, I'm following you."

"Now, I know you might not love hearing this, but just like you should strive to be as clear as possible with everything you can, you should also strive to be as consistent as you can with as many things as possible." Dan paused again as if he were trying to gauge Marty's thoughts and then added, "With that being said, like the building blocks and big-ticket items that should be a focus of clarity, there are certain ways you must strive to be consistent. Consistency in these areas will help you become the best leader you possibly can and create a work environment where people can perform at their best. When you're consistent as a leader, others will follow your example."

Dan then took the cap off the pen and added this to the whiteboard:

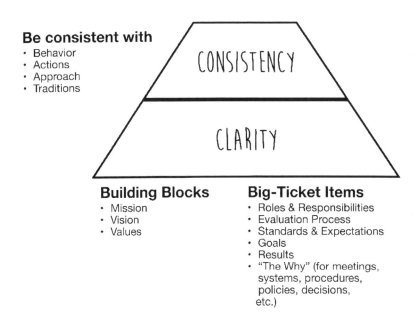

Be consistent with
- Behavior
- Actions
- Approach
- Traditions

CONSISTENCY

CLARITY

Building Blocks
- Mission
- Vision
- Values

Big-Ticket Items
- Roles & Responsibilities
- Evaluation Process
- Standards & Expectations
- Goals
- Results
- "The Why" (for meetings, systems, procedures, policies, decisions, etc.)

Marty looked at what Dan had written. He was still very intrigued by the second C. Dan interrupted his thoughts again by saying as he walked back to his chair, "Your level of consistency at work will actually lower stress levels around the office to an optimal level. When people know what to expect from their leader, they can perform. On the flip side, if you keep people guessing, it will paralyze them from making decisions and moving forward. Thus consistency in that first item on the list, your behavior, is vital." Dan nodded toward the whiteboard.

"I'm not sure I completely understand," Marty responded honestly.

"Let me see if I can help make it clearer," Dan said, moving forward in his chair.

"The first thing that needs to be consistent is your personal behavior and attitude. Too many bosses I've hung around demonstrate very different behaviors and attitudes based on their moods and the emotions of the moment. They come across to their teams as very hot and cold, or yin and yang, or salt and pepper, if you know what I mean."

Marty laughed, and Dan smiled. Marty thought he did understand what Dan meant. Dan went on, "One day the leader may be pleasant, easy to approach, and all smiles, and the next day they seem angry, bothered, and annoyed by anything and everything. And this might not be day to day but even hour by hour."

While Marty thought about that, Dan pushed on. "Being a leader is stressful, so it's easy to see why leaders can be so inconsistent with their behaviors and attitudes. It's natural, really. But to positively influence your team, you must learn to control your emotions. You must show up the same way every day, regardless of what's going on or what's just happened. In the most stressful moments at work, your people need to know they can count on you. And you can create this sense of security by being consistent."

Marty liked the sound of consistency and felt he knew what Dan meant by it when he asked, "Have you ever worked for a boss like this? Who seemed hot and cold? Who seemed to have a different attitude from day to day?"

Without thought, Marty rolled his eyes after hearing Dan's question. Realizing what he had done and the perception it might create, he quickly tried to recover and simply nodded and said, "Yes." Marty could feel his cheeks turning red as Dan smiled.

Now chuckling a bit, Dan said, "OK, I'm guessing it's safe to say you've worked for someone who was a little inconsistent in the past. Really, this isn't too surprising to me. Most of us have."

To say that Marty's first boss at Wiser Care had been like this felt like an understatement to Marty. He was a hard driver and got things done and even had the approval of his superiors. But for Marty, he turned work life into a living nightmare. Marty never knew what to expect from him each day he came to work. One day this boss would behave as if he was Marty's best friend, and the next day Marty wondered if he thought he was the most incompetent person who had ever worked for him. On good days, Marty dreamed about being promoted or earning a raise, but on bad days, he was certain he was soon to be fired.

Because of this erratic behavior on the part of his boss, Marty was constantly nervous at work; in fact, the whole team was. He had just graduated at the top of his MBA class at a pretty good business school and had turned down other attractive employment opportunities to join Wiser Care because of his desire to work in health care, but now he was feeling so unsure of himself. Marty had to admit this boss rocked his confidence a little. He remembered becoming extremely guarded and careful at work. Then, after only a few months, Marty began searching for a new job outside the organization. Though he considered himself to be a very committed person,

.e couldn't take his boss's unpredictable behavior
. e.

Before he could land something new, however, things suddenly changed. After a few very stressful months at work with many sleepless nights, Marty received what felt like at the time some of the best news of his life. His boss was being promoted, and he would soon report to a new supervisor. Marty could not have been more relieved. He often hoped he'd never experience something like that again. Unfortunately, though never as extreme as his first boss, Marty found that many of his bosses acted in similar ways. This unpredictability always drove him a little crazy, but he had learned how to mostly ignore it.

Lost in thought, Marty was suddenly brought back to the present moment as Dan continued. "As leaders, we often undervalue the impact our behaviors and attitudes have on others. The truth is, the impact is very real. When people believe you hold the future of their career in your hands, how you behave and what you say and do will be scrutinized and overanalyzed. You have to understand that as a leader, you're constantly on stage.

"Too many leaders fail to realize how much their attitude or simple comments or actions affect others. Too many leaders lose credibility in the eyes of those they lead by making simple off-the-wall comments, acting in unpredictable ways, and, well, being inconsistent."

Dan had Marty's full attention now. Once again, he knew firsthand the impact of an inconsistent boss, as Dan had labeled it, and he knew the effect this could have on those they led.

"Inconsistency causes unproductive tension, stress, and worry. As a result, the boss does not get the best from his team. I've seen this happen time and time again. It's sad, Marty."

Marty could tell Dan seriously felt sad about it. Both moved slightly in their chairs when Dan looked again at Marty and said, "The reason this is often the most difficult *C* to establish is because we are human beings; we are inconsistent and emotional creatures and not robots. However, as a boss, you have to strive to be consistent. Your behavior and attitude must be consistent each day. Your responses to problems must be consistent; your mood every morning should be consistent; how you handle yourself, how you interact with others, and how you feel about people whether they are a housekeeper or a physician must be consistent."

Marty's mind instantly went to Roger, whom Dan had introduced him to on Monday morning. Marty could tell Dan felt the same about Roger as he did about Dr. Simpson, for example. He wondered if this was what Dan meant. He decided it must be.

Dan continued now, interrupting Marty's thoughts. "You won't be perfect at it, and no one expects that of you, but your team will appreciate and notice your efforts. They'll respond well to your consistent behavior. And if you can provide that sort of stability and security to your team, they'll be able to maximize their efforts. They'll produce more for you than they otherwise would, and that will make you happy. Times will be stressful and hard; I know you know that. You may even have difficult challenges outside work, but you must strive to provide stability for your team. You must provide consistency. Without it, work just isn't as safe a place as it should be. No one likes working for an erratic boss."

Marty thought Dan might be finished with his thought when he casually added, "In fact, being consistently angry or rude or having a bad attitude is better than changing how you behave each day."

Both Marty's eyebrows raised up at that thought. Dan seemed to notice and went on.

"I'm serious, Marty. It would be better to work for you knowing how you are, even if it were rude or unreasonable, than to not be sure what you were going to get every day. You have to remember that, in their eyes, you hold their future and their career in your hands. This inherently causes some level of nervousness and stress around you, but when you add to it by being someone who is unpredictable, it can totally sour your effectiveness as a leader and amp up these distracting feelings.

"Being rude consistently, day in and day out, for example, as terrible as it may sound, would still ease these negative emotions of uncertainty among your team members because they would learn to cope and adjust to your behavior. They'd come to know what to expect out of you and would find ways to work around it. But…" Dan paused for a moment as if to add emphasis to what he was about to say. "It's impossible to adjust to someone who changes their tune every day. Frankly, it's hard to work for someone who is volatile."

And with that, Marty leaned back in his chair, surprised. This was something he had certainly never considered.

Hit Home

Dan stood and stretched his back again, which allowed Marty to have a moment of reflection about what he had said.

"I see why this is so difficult," Marty responded almost more to himself while quietly thinking about his wife, April. He recalled only about a month ago, she had complained to him that she never knew what to expect from him after work. Sometimes he seemed enthusiastic and happy, and other times he was almost depressed and emotionless as she saw it. Though she hadn't used Dan's exact word, this inconsistency in his behavior made it very difficult for her. She never knew how to react and respond to him, she'd said. She'd even shared that she found herself always being guarded and careful around him. Though it had stung for a moment, Marty was grateful she had been honest with him. He cherished their relationship, and he promised to be better, though he had to admit not much had changed. But now it dawned on him in this moment that he was being like his first boss at Wiser Care toward his wife in some ways. He couldn't believe it. As the blood rushed from his face, Marty thought to himself, *Could I end up behaving like my first boss toward my new team?* He quickly pushed the thought aside and vowed it would never happen.

"Now, I don't want you to think I'm giving you permission to participate in poor behavior every day," Dan quipped, lightening the mood a little bit as he laughed. Marty wondered if Dan could perceive his uneasy feelings. "We all have things we can improve, and we should always be striving to be better, but hopefully, that means some consistent progress and not the boomerang affect I'm talking about here where we go from one extreme in our behavior and attitudes to another and then back again. When people know what to expect from their boss each day, they can perform. Consistency provides a sense of predictability and reliability at work. This creates feelings of security and trust. Just as each of us has a desire to see clearly, we also all crave a level of stability."

"Wait a second," Marty said, snapping out of his worrisome thoughts. Pretending to be thinking about this more seriously, he said, "So you're saying it's OK for me to miss work and go golfing every Friday as long as I'm consistent at doing it, right? Like every Friday instead of only two out of the four or five Fridays in the month because that would just upset people, right?" Marty was trying to keep a straight face, but he was unsuccessful at holding off a smile when Dan looked up.

Marty could tell that, for a split second, Dan was worried before he realized Marty was joking again. He enjoyed pulling Dan's leg, especially when it felt like they could use a good laugh.

"Maybe not exactly." Dan smiled. "But what I will say is that if you can successfully implement these four C's, your people will make you look good and support you in just about anything you choose to do. And trust me, it will allow for more enjoyable golf."

"If that's true," Marty said, trying to look serious again, "then I guess I better start paying attention. What did you say the first C is again?" He held his pen and notepad close to his chest as if he were just now ready to write something important down. Again his attempt to remain straight faced failed, and Dan laughed out loud this time.

Marty hoped Dan appreciated his sarcastic comments, though he couldn't tell for sure. After a moment, Dan regained his composure and said, "After our initial phone conversations, I didn't expect this from you. To be honest, I can be a little too buttoned up sometimes. I imagine you never could have guessed it." Both smiled before Dan added, "I think the team is going to appreciate some more humor around here. I think you'll be a great fit with them, Marty." Marty felt Dan was being honest and appreciated his kind remarks. Just when he was feeling good, Dan said, looking and sounding serious again, "If you will ever let me finish this second *C*."

For a split second, Marty worried Dan was a little upset, until Dan smiled widely. Marty realized Dan had gotten him back and laughed.

Clarity in Action

"Let me ask you something, Marty," Dan said as he regained his composure and interrupted Marty's laughter. "Now, I'm sure they taught you everything about business at that hoity-toity school of yours, but do you know one major reason why McDonald's has been so successful over so many years? You know the place I'm talking about, right, like, over a gazillion burgers sold, give or take a few?" Dan said with some sarcasm in his voice again.

Marty sat up now, a little confused at the change in course of their conversation. "I know it's always tried to acquire the very best real estate, right? Is that it?" He responded hesitantly, feeling a little embarrassed that it might not be the right answer.

"I'm sure that's another big contributing factor for its success over the years, but it's not the reason I'm thinking about." Marty could sense Dan had decided his question wasn't very fair as he could see he was about to give him the answer. "What I'm referring to is…" Dan paused for a moment as if to give his answer a more dramatic effect before saying, "…consistency."

Of course, Marty thought to himself. *Obviously!*

Dan went on. "You see, whether you like McDonald's products or not, you always know what you're going to get. There's no guessing, no wondering, and no uncertainty. When I pull up to a drive-through window, I know exactly what to expect. McDonald's french fries are the same whether I'm in Kentucky or Maine. Its Big Mac is the same in Florida and California. Its chicken nuggets, for better or worse, are the same in Chicago as in Dallas. McDonald's has always done a good job, a remarkable job, actually, at duplicating its products no matter where you are. Its consistency over the years is amazing when you stop and think about the thousands of locations it has served food across the world. Consistency is a huge driver of its worldwide success. Whether you like McDonald's food or not, you can always rely on the consistency of its products."

Dan waited for a second and then continued. "Great bosses and great organizations are the same. They are like McDonald's of sorts. They consistently provide the same behavior, tell the same stories, beat the same drum, and do the same things day in and day out. They reinforce their clarity by being consistent. Where clarity may be more about the message and communicating it over and over again, consistency is about behaviors and action. In a way, consistency is your clarity in action."

Though he hadn't said anything, Marty was glad Dan had brought up clarity. Marty had thought about the similarities between the first two C's during their discussion. Now was a perfect time to ask. "Can you explain your last point a little more?"

"Sure. In fact, I'm really glad you asked because there's overlap between these two C's, but they're different. Clarity is the information we share in our communication. It's what we communicate that's important to us, such as why we do what we do and how we are going to do it. Consistency is the action; it's the actual doing. We clarify our core values, for example, but then we strive to consistently live them and make decision based on them. We clarify our processes, and then we consistently do them. We clarify the type of individuals we want working for us, and then we consistently hire those kinds of individuals. We clarify our goals, and then we consistently measure them and work to reach them. I like to think of consistency as being the follow-through to clarity. Without it, clarity can lose much of its power. Because even if I say our core value is honesty until I'm blue in the face, if I'm not consistently behaving in an honest way, the clarity I've created won't be very helpful."

Marty was intrigued. What Dan was sharing was certainly nothing he had learned in business school. Sure, he had taken dozens of leadership workshops and classes, but he couldn't recall ever being lectured on consistency and clarity like this. Spoken, it seemed so obvious.

"Are you beginning to understand the difference?" Dan asked, watching Marty closely.

Marty felt he understood, but he still wondered why every leader didn't do this. *Why isn't clarity and consistency emphasized more in leadership courses?*, he thought.

Then, almost as if reading his mind, Dan continued. "It may sound easy, but it's not. You yourself have said today that clarity and consistency have not always been normal practices by your previous supervisors, and unfortunately, most of the organizations around the world don't stress these concepts to their leaders enough, if at all. This is sad because too many eager and capable leaders end up failing. The four *C*'s model gives you a framework to focus your leadership efforts. It invites you to constantly consider those things that will make you most successful, those things that will add the most value as a leader. Many leaders fail at establishing clarity and consistency because they're rarely stressed as being important. And if they're never brought up or taught to leaders, then how can we expect them to really hone in on them and strive be good at them?"

Marty thought Dan had a good point. Then Dan added, "Besides, as we talked about earlier, it also requires a lot of discipline. It takes discipline to do things consistently. But the effort is worth it. It is always worth it.

"When people feel a sense of security at work that only consistency can provide, they are able to produce and engage at much higher levels. Work becomes a much better place to them. The bottom line is consistency and clarity help you produce results."

Dan leaned back, and the two sat in silence for a moment. Marty was thinking about the importance of the first two C's when he noticed Dan suddenly furrowing his brow. Marty was about to ask if he was worried about something when Dan said, "I'm concerned that as I talk about consistency, it may sound like you have to be a robot without emotions. Please understand that's not it at all, Marty. We are human, and we must be human. So consistency is not about eliminating fun, emotion, or excitement. It's not about avoiding feelings of disappointment, frustration, or discouragement. And it certainly is not about never changing things up, being spontaneous, or surprising your team every once in a while. It's really nothing of the sort.

"I hope you don't misunderstand what I've told you. Consistency is simply about a disciplined, steady approach that people can come to rely on. It's about being someone who can be counted on in good times and in bad. It's about being relentless about what matters most to the team and the organization, even if everything else needs to change. It's about treating others kindly whether things are going well or not so well. Your people need to know they can depend on the person who holds much of their future and success in the organization in their hands. Once they learn they can depend on you, you'll begin to earn their trust and respect. And once you have their trust and respect, there's almost nothing you can ask of them that they won't do with every ounce of effort."

Marty liked the sound of that. Dan went on. "We're all going to feel emotion, and we should. I think for consistency to really take root in your center, though, you need to be honest about that emotion—you need to be clear about what is making you upset or excited or whatever the emotion may be. When people have that clarity, they'll be understanding and come to know what to expect from you when similar circumstances arise.

"For example, if it drives you crazy any time someone shows up late for a meeting, and you know it shows, you need to talk about it. Share with the team that it drives you crazy when people are late because it is disrespectful to others. Be clear about why it makes you angry and what your expectation is. Do this consistently in an honest and open way, and people will respond."

Marty thought this made a lot of sense, and he was excited about what he was learning. But he still had one burning question that had been growing into a really big concern.

A Big Concern

"I do have a question about consistency," Marty said with a furrowed brow. "I've been at Wiser Care for many years now, and it seems to me a lot has changed. And a lot of these changes in my mind have been very good for our organization. For example, moving to electronic medical records from the old paper kind has been great. Or the data and metrics we have access to now when compared to when I started seems extremely helpful in running a good operation. So, are you saying that the company shouldn't have changed? That it should have stayed more consistent?"

Dan eyes opened wide for a second and he quickly shook his head. "No, Marty, that's not what I'm saying at all. Thank you for asking the question." Marty could tell Dan meant it.

"Consistency is not about never changing—heaven knows we must change frequently to stay ahead of the competition and to meet the needs of our customers. Change is inevitable and necessary. We have to change!" Dan said with emphasis. "What consistency is about in this model is how you deal with change. Your approach to change can be consistent and provide a sense of dependability in the midst of a ton of moving parts. Likewise, your consistent behavior, attitude, and actions toward change will provide what your team needs in order to feel safe, even with rapid and frequent changes all around them. In health care, you know we're all about change."

Marty definitely agreed with that last statement, but he wasn't completely sure if he was grasping what Dan was saying and hoped he'd share more. Thankfully, Dan quickly continued.

"Let me try to share an example of what I mean. A good friend of mine worked as a CEO for Wiser Care for a short while at a smaller health care center. He was a great guy but struggled with the constant changes in health care—they drove him crazy. Anyway, one year our reimbursement system got flipped upside down. This came a few months after the company decided to downsize therapy staff based on the old reimbursement system. Though that change to downsize therapy staff wasn't easy, my friend rallied his team and made it clear to all of them why the change was necessary and how it could help them improve. He even sought feedback from important members of his leadership team on how to best implement the necessary changes. He really did a great job with this difficult change, and his team supported him.

"However, a few months later when it came time to evolve and adjust to the new reimbursement system, my friend took a very different approach. First he ignored it and acted as if the change wasn't really going to happen, even though everyone on his team knew about it. Then he talked about how ridiculous the change to the reimbursement system was and how he didn't agree with it. He complained about it constantly, and if I recall, he even thought he'd find ways around it. Finally, he reluctantly made changes to adjust to the reimbursement system, but he didn't involve his team, and he continued to grumble about it."

Dan now paused for a moment and looked at Marty. "Based on what I've told you so far, how do you think his team will feel the next time there are more changes in the industry?"

Marty thought about the question for a moment and answered, "I'm not sure. Some might think he'd behave like he did when the therapy staff reductions were necessary, and others might worry he'd react like he did with the changes to the reimbursement system. I guess they wouldn't be sure what to expect."

"Exactly," said Dan. "No one could predict how my friend would react to the next change. His approach toward change was very inconsistent. Every time a new change came along, he behaved differently, and this really had a negative effect on his team."

Marty thought he understood when Dan offered, "If he'd taken the same approach with the change in the reimbursement system that he did when he downsized his therapy staff, and followed the same approach again with the next industry change, he would have eventually built a level of consistency and dependability for his team toward change. This would have produced feelings of security in spite of the many changes they'd be dealing with. Do you see why the consistency in how we approach things, such as changes in the industry, dealing with a difficult employee, handling customer complaints, interacting with physicians, or responding to poor clinical outcomes, matters?

Marty nodded and felt he was beginning to understand. He could better see how consistency in his behaviors, actions, and approach would help his leadership and reinforce clarity. He could see why it mattered so much. He also could perceive how, in a lot of ways, the leader of a team would set the tone for consistency for the entire group.

Breaking Marty's thoughts again, Dan said, "Much like our behaviors, how we react to and approach similar situations that come our way in the workplace matters. We should be consistent. For example, ignoring the fact that someone missed an important leadership meeting one time and then becoming highly upset the next time someone misses the same meeting is an inconsistent approach to the same situation. Or not reacting when you notice a nurse who didn't wash her hands after care, and then the next time terminating an employee who you observe not washing their hands after care. Can you see how nervous your people can become in an inconsistent environment like this? These are true examples of things I've observed leaders do, and this inconsistency can drive a team crazy."

Marty knew he had observed similar inconsistent approaches by leaders. Dan added, "An inconsistent approach to similar situations can really squash trust and hurt your credibility as a leader."

Marty's head was now reeling. This made perfect sense, but he worried he hadn't paid enough attention to the first two *C*'s in his previous management positions. As Marty worried about whether he had approached things consistently in the past, Dan said, "Marty, though we don't think this way often, consistency is a strategic decision a leader must consciously make. They must decide it's important, and then they must commit to putting forth an effort to be consistent."

Marty liked that thought and decided there wasn't much he could do about the past. He reasoned that all he could do now was to commit to being as consistent as he possibly could be moving forward.

With a break in the conversation, Marty decided to share a thought that summarized what Dan had said. "We all like to be around people who we believe are consistent because they're the people we feel we can count on and trust. It's logical then that those are the people we're most willing to follow."

"Precisely!" Dan said, nodding in agreement.

Marty certainly wanted his team members to want to follow him. He wanted them to feel safe and secure at work because he knew what it felt like when your boss wasn't very consistent.

Marty could see why consistency was the second *C* in Dan's model to successful leadership.

More Examples

Dan turned and looked over his shoulder at the board. Marty wondered what he was looking for. He turned back to face Marty. He put his right hand to his chin as if he were considering something. After another moment, he said, "Let me share a few more things with you, Marty, that have to do with establishing consistency."

"Sounds good," Marty responded quickly, and Dan went on.

"Many, many years ago..." Marty noticed a smile forming at the corner of Dan's mouth. Dan waited for a moment as if he were checking to see if Marty would make a sarcastic comment. Marty resisted the urge this time, and Dan continued. "Before coming here to Wiser, I worked for a company and a supervisor who changed things up just for the sake of change. At least that's what it felt like. For example, one day nothing was more important than sales, the next day it was to improve customer service, the next was to grow and acquire new business, and then the next it was safety in the workplace. And if that wasn't bad enough, he even changed what he called certain things. For example, he had core objectives that then became strategic initiatives, and then they were called company pillars. As you might guess, this created confusion as well as what felt like a very volatile environment. I remember personally feeling I couldn't count on anything at that company. Each day I drove in to work, I wasn't sure what to expect. It really was quite stressful, and the turnover at the company was very high for good reason. There was little to no security and stability. There was so little consistency."

Marty nodded as he could see how such an environment could be hard on any team.

"Now, although that was bad, what was even worse was how often the leadership team, including my boss, rolled out new initiatives, programs, policies, systems, you name it. My boss at the time was a gifted speaker. His rollout speeches were often inspiring and motivating, but then there was never any follow-through, and the exciting new initiatives or systems would never last."

Marty nodded again; all this sounded too familiar to him.

"For example, one year we were going to get a little bonus each month there were no employee injuries at work, and the dollar amount of this bonus was supposed to grow each consecutive month we went without an injury. This sounded like a good idea to me since it was an area we had struggled with. I knew it sounded great to many of our staff members who could really use the extra cash."

Dan leaned back now, relaxing in his chair. "Well, if I remember right, the first month we had an injury, so we were told we wouldn't get a bonus, which was fine; that was the program. The next month we did go injury free, and I believe everyone did receive a bonus, but after that, it rarely was mentioned again. People would ask me if we were getting a bonus or if there'd been an injury, and I had to tell them I honestly didn't know. My boss at the time would put off questions about it and soon acted as if the program never existed. This was a common pattern, and it caused a lot of dissatisfaction among our team. Soon, no matter what the next great speech was about, everyone knew we'd eventually go back to doing things the way we had always done them."

Marty could relate to Dan's story; he'd heard his fair share of great "kickoff" speeches, only to see the new initiatives and programs fade away. *This is all too common, even at Wiser Care,* he thought. He could even picture in his mind everyone's eyes rolling as he shared something new that his prior boss wanted to roll out. Just like the many others that proceeded it, Marty's team knew it wouldn't last. As he thought about this, Marty did find it irritating and always hated how he felt it made him look to his team. Thankfully, his team mostly understood he was taking directions from his boss.

Dan continued. "Inconsistency really hurt the credibility and trust we had in both our boss and the organization."

Marty realized the level of trust he'd had in his prior boss had been greatly diminished by similar behaviors. "Good speeches with no follow-through get old pretty quick," Marty commented, almost to himself.

"That's true," Dan agreed, moving forward in his chair again.

Looking at Marty seriously, he said, "Don't do this, Marty. Don't be inconsistent in this way. If you decide to give a bonus for no injuries during the year, then do it. If you say you are going to review individual goals with your direct reports once a month, then do it. If you decide you want to establish a weekly meeting schedule, then follow it. And if you know you aren't so good at following a schedule or need more flexibility, then please don't ever mention it. The same is true with programs and initiatives and policies and systems. If you don't have the discipline to follow through and do them, then don't ever mention it."

Marty sat back, listening to what Dan was saying. He thought it all seemed obvious, yet most of the leaders he had worked under had done what Dan was sharing to a certain extent.

"Think things through before introducing them to your team. Know how you will follow up and follow through with what you are about to introduce before you ever announce it. Make sure it's something you plan to do and have the ability to really stick with for a period of time. Make sure it's something that will truly help your center. Don't be a boss who is all talk with no follow-through. Being consistent in this way will help you be a good boss."

Marty agreed with this, then asked, "What if you were sure the program would work, but then you realize down the road it was a mistake. Should you stick with it for consistency's sake?"

Dan didn't take long to answer. "No, you shouldn't. If you know you've made a mistake, own it and clearly let people know you made a mistake. Tell them why you're now stopping or changing something you rolled out. Without this clarity around why you're moving on or stopping or changing something, people will just believe you're being inconsistent. However, if you clearly explain "the why" or the reason for the change, people will hear what you're saying and won't chalk it up to unreliability or think you can't be trusted to follow through. This is important. Too many leaders brush off programs without clearly sharing the reason why, and then their people are left to wonder if they can be trusted."

Marty relaxed his hands and put them on the desk. This made a lot of sense in his mind, and he really liked the idea of being a consistent boss.

Dan then added, "Remember, consistency and clarity build on each other. You need one to help support the other. If what we say is most important to us changes each day, or if how we ask our people to behave changes each day, or if duties and responsibilities are constantly moving around, or if we are frequently introducing new programs without following through on them, people are going to lose interest, be con-fused, and ultimately withhold trust. When clarity and consistency are lacking, becoming highly successful as a leader becomes virtually impossible.

"However, if you can clarify things by consistently talking about the things that matter most, if you can consistently do the small things that will help the business move forward, if you can consistently behave in a way that helps people feel cared about and valued, if you can consistently stick to the programs you introduce, if you can consistently approach similar situations in similar ways, if you can talk the talk and then walk the walk, then the opposite will be true. People will feel they have a stable work environment and a leader they can count on. With high levels of clarity and consistency, becoming a great leader is almost inevitable."

Marty liked the sound of that. In the past he had often envisioned himself walking the halls of a center as a CEO with his head held high being proud of the team he was leading and the good work they were doing. At this moment this vision flashed through is mind. Now more than ever, he was ready to do all he could to implement the first two C's to leadership success.

Dan stood up for a minute and stretched. He looked at Marty and said, "Let's take a quick break, but before we do, let me just add that consistency does take a lot of discipline, and you have to constantly work at it. And your team will cut you some slack when you have a bad day here and there, because trust me, you will from time to time. We all do. If you try to be as consistent as possible with your behaviors, attitude, actions, and approach, though, you will create a safe haven for your team. And the reality is that for some of your staff, work may be the only safe haven they have."

The gravity of his responsibilities as a boss hit him with a force he never anticipated. Marty always knew being a supervisor would be important and could affect the lives of those who worked under him, but he felt with Dan he was seeing more clearly the stewardship that came with being a leader. He then thought about how his bosses in the past had influenced and impacted his life for better or worse. Marty wanted to be the boss who would make life better for his employees and their families. *But how?* This question made him panic for a split second and then... *The four* C's, he thought, shaking his head as he realized how helpful this information was to him. If he could focus on the four *C's*, he knew they would lead him to success as a leader.

Dan again interrupted his thoughts. "I'm going to run down the hall; let's start back up in ten minutes." He whooshed out the door and left Marty alone to reflect more on what he was learning.

Personal Story

Dan walked through the door without knocking, and Marty decided it was time to have a little fun with him again. "Hey, you didn't knock," he said, trying to look upset.

Marty could see Dan wasn't buying it this time. Dan must have decided to even the score a bit because he said, "Well, I just got off the phone with my wife, and we've decided together that I should stay. So I guess this is now my office again."

Dan seemed sincere, which made Marty wonder, horrified, whether he was actually telling the truth, but then Dan began to laugh. "My heart almost skipped a beat," Marty said, putting a hand on his chest. "You can't do that to me right now, Dan. I have enough stress in my life as it is." Both continued to laugh together and joked around for a few minutes, enjoying each other's company.

Eventually, Dan sat back in his usual spot and looked seriously at Marty. "Do you mind if I share one more personal story with you?" he asked, sounding and looking almost somber.

"Not at all," Marty responded, moving forward in his chair. "I'd love you to."

"About twenty-five years ago, something happened in my life that truly made me a believer in this second C. I'd been a CEO for just over three years at my first center and was having great success. It was my first time being in charge and leading an entire center, and the thrill and excitement of it all was really indescribable. I loved it! For three years I'd worked closely with my team, and we really had some amazing success together."

Marty had heard the stories about Dan and his success even early on in his career with Wiser. Marty was sure Dan had earned his reputation in those first few years of great achievement as a CEO and then had only continued to build on his legacy from there. He sat forward, eager to hear more.

"I loved my team, Marty. We were an all-star team in my mind, and because of them, I looked good. I was really lucky to work with them."

Marty doubted Dan was the only one who was lucky in that situation. Marty was about to say so, but Dan continued quickly.

"Anyway, something happened to me. I'm not sure what triggered it, but I stopped thinking straight. I stopped doing the things that had helped my team become successful. I relaxed and must have believed we'd always be successful, regardless of what I did. I became a leader without consistency, although I didn't realize that was my problem at the time."

Marty continued to listen intently intrigued by Dan's story.

"Looking back later, though, I could see how I had slowly stopped doing the little things that helped me be an effective leader. First it was my actions and approach to things, and then it was my behavior, and finally it was my attitude. As you might guess, my team slowly began to deteriorate, and I blamed them for it." Dan shook his head, somber again. "How deceived was I?"

Marty wanted to say something but wasn't sure exactly what, so he decided to let Dan continue and not interrupt his thoughts.

"The truth was it wasn't because of them but because of me and my level of inconsistency and unpredictability. This began to show up throughout the health care center because of how I was acting and behaving. Hindsight is always twenty-twenty."

Dan sighed and paused for a moment. Marty again wondered if he should say something, but then Dan continued, looking troubled. "I've wondered over the years if the team would have been better off if I had just resigned. Sadly, the inconsistency I created eventually led to the breakup of our all-star team, and within time I was reassigned to another health care center. Well, this one, in fact."

Marty was caught completely off guard by what Dan had shared. As he was trying to wrap his head around it, Dan added, "In a lot of ways, my being reassigned here was a leap of faith for the organization and saved my career at Wiser Care. Because of consistency or the lack thereof during this difficult time, I went from being a rising star in the organization to almost a has-been. Those were hard days for me—a hard lesson to learn."

Marty couldn't believe what he was hearing. An array of emotions went through him. First, he felt bad for Dan and couldn't imagine how anyone could expect him to be consistent all the time. Next, he felt a little angry at Dan's team for not stepping up and doing their part. Finally, he felt shock that Dan had messed up to the point where he needed to be reassigned to another center. Marty had heard that Dan did go through a short rough patch during his time at Wiser Care, but he really hadn't believed it. Or at least he'd assumed it wasn't really a big deal. He certainly never imagined he'd been asked to leave his position and move to another center. This story really threw Marty for a loop.

After gathering his composure some, Marty asked, "Can you tell me more about what you stopped doing?" Marty wanted to know. He needed to learn all he could from Dan and avoid making the same mistake. He could also sense how much the situation still hurt Dan, so he wanted to be sensitive.

"Absolutely," Dan replied, sounding a little more upbeat. "Like I said, reflecting back, it was inconsistency in my actions and approach that led to my demise. I began rescheduling and showing up late for important meetings, for example, and let small things go that I would have normally addressed and corrected right away. I stopped having regular meetings with my core team of leaders, and I got bored repeating and reviewing the goals and results of our center. Though I didn't know it at the time, I began delegating some of my most important responsibilities to others, such as presenting in new employee orientations on the mission, vision, and values and involving myself in the interview process. I had done such a good job getting to know my staff but let that go. Sooner than I thought possible, I saw mostly strangers working at my center. I also stopped reviewing my budgets religiously and closely monitoring key clinical metrics. These are a handful of things that come to mind. I was so consistent on them for so long and then just began to stop doing them. We had a lot of success, and I guess I decided I could just coast, socialize with physicians and peers, and participate only in what I believed were the most enjoyable parts of the job. I obviously didn't recognize how consistency had helped me be a good leader for my team."

Marty was blown away that Dan had stopped doing these things that seemed to have helped him achieve incredible results. Though he had seen others be inconsistent, it wasn't something he ever expected from Dan, even if it had been well over twenty years ago.

Dan went on. "To add to this, as our results slowly declined, it affected how I behaved and interacted with my people. Soon my attitude became more erratic as I began to blame others for our slow decline. Oh, I'd apologize from time to time, but then another poor number would come out, and I'd go off on my team again. Eventually, people didn't know what to expect from me, and we began to lose important staff. I could feel the wheels coming off, and others noticed as well and began to jump ship. Looking back, I firmly believe that my sudden inconsistency slowly eroded away what we had built."

"Wow," Marty whispered under his breath. He really had a hard time envisioning Dan behaving in this way. Despite his story, Marty felt Dan was the prime example of consistency based on all he had observed and heard about him.

"Looking back now, I think I just got cocky and complacent. My people were so capable and supported me wholeheartedly, but I stopped being who I had been for them to that point. I have full confidence they would have continued to reach new heights had I stuck with this *C*. If I understood back then what I do now, I can only hope I would have been more vigilant at staying consistent. With the knowledge of the model, I think I would have recognized it and improved. I learned an invaluable lesson from this experience. Do you see why this is so important?"

Marty was still taken aback by what Dan shared. "I certainly do see how critical consistency is and really appreciate you sharing this story with me." Marty realized that for Dan, this was a lesson learned that had served him well over the next twenty years of his career. Clearly, he hadn't made the same mistake again.

Marty was thankful once again that Dan was passing his most painful lessons learned on to him. He felt he was gaining invaluable knowledge from his newfound mentor.

Traditions

Dan looked at his watch and said, "Time sure does go by fast. It's later than I realized. I apologize for taking up so much of your time already."

At that moment Marty looked at the clock on the wall behind Dan and wanted to encourage him to stay. He wanted to learn all he could about the four C's now; he didn't want to wait. Marty knew he was being impatient and thought better of saying what he was thinking. He realized he should be more grateful Dan was willing to spend his first few mornings of retirement with him.

"Don't worry about my time, Dan. I really should be thanking you more. I'm sure you never imagined this is how your first couple of days of retirement would go."

Dan smiled and said honestly, "No, it's not, but I'm happy to do it. There's nothing I want more than for you and the team here to succeed."

Marty could tell Dan meant it. Then Dan added, "And I know the four C's model can really help."

Marty nodded in agreement. He was so impressed with Dan and his respect for him seemed to grow with each passing minute.

Dan, twisting awkwardly, pointed to the whiteboard behind him. "Let's talk about the last part of consistency, which is also very important. Another way to solidify consistency is by establishing traditions." Turning back to face Marty he continued, "I guess you could say consistency and traditions go hand in hand."

Marty looked at Dan, a little unsure of what he meant. Dan added, "What I mean is when you do things consistently, they become a part of who you are. For example, we did our daily morning huddles that I told you about consistently. After time, it became a way of doing business for us. We don't even think twice about doing it now; it's a morning tradition. It's just part of how we do things around here and something people can depend on."

Marty thought that made sense.

"When we consistently do things, we create our own unique way of doing business. This builds a sense of belonging within your team and organization. Without consistency, your way of doing business wouldn't become clear and so in a lot of ways wouldn't exist at all. It's hard to establish a strong, recognizable, and unique culture without consistency and traditions. Do you remember the extra page we added to our employment application to increase clarity?" Dan asked.

Marty nodded, remembering how Dan and his team had created this additional page to help them clarify from the very beginning what was most important to their center.

"The one where we ask those applying to answer questions about our mission and values?"

"Yes, I remember," Marty said.

"Though I may have mentioned this briefly, that has become the most important document we review during our interview process. It has shaped the way we structure our interviews. We focus many of our questions around that specific page. It's what we do during interviews; it's our own unique way of doing business. Consistency has helped us create a tradition of how we conduct interviews."

Marty understood what Dan was talking about. One thing that made Wiser Care unique was the way it allowed its CEOs to operate its health care centers. Rather than setting up strict policies on how things had to be done in each center, it allowed CEOs a lot of latitude to make decisions and do things that were best based on the centers' unique local communities. Not being tied to a one-size-fits-all approach was the way the organization did business, and it attracted a lot of good leaders who wanted more flexibility in running their own operations. In Marty's mind, this was probably an example of a company tradition or how Wiser Care did business.

Dan looked up toward the corner of the room for a moment and then back at Marty. "There are other kinds of traditions you should actively strive to establish as well to improve consistency. These are more 'fun' traditions. For example, we started a holiday gift exchange between our department heads about nine years back, and it's become something we do each year. It's become a tradition that encourages us to take an interest in one another and spend some time relaxing in a more comfortable, stress-free setting. Our people really look forward to it each year, and it's something they can count on. It's become a part of our unique traditions.

"During that time of year our department head team also nominates and adopts a few families to care for. We ensure these families have a great holiday by gathering gifts and providing everything they need for a nice meal. Typically, the families we choose are members of our own staff who need a little extra help during the holidays. This is truly a comforting tradition that brings a lot of joy on a lot of different levels.

"We also have a springtime family and community barbecue. As you might imagine, this is always a big hit. People look forward to it each year, and it's another tradition that shows we value relationships."

117

Marty could see how establishing traditions helped reinforce feelings of consistency, stability, and connection.

Dan then smiled and said, "Now, this one may sound silly." His smile grew as he continued talking. "But here at our health care center, we always serve *only* green punch at all of our parties and events. Honestly, I'm not sure when this tradition began. Since our center's brand color is green, at some point in time, it's what we started to do, and it's stuck. And let me warn you now, if you bring or even try to provide a different color punch at any function here, the team will get after you!"

Dan chuckled as Marty smiled and considered why this really mattered.

"Even these little things that seem so insignificant can reinforce consistency and create a unique culture your people can count on. As you create traditions, people begin to look forward to them, and it helps create feelings of stability and belonging."

Marty thought he understood Dan's point on traditions and liked the idea of creating a unique way of doing things through consistency. He saw how inconsistency would really destroy any hope of developing a unique culture that people could get excited about.

Dan glanced at his watch again, then, looking as if he were considering something, said, "I promise I'm almost done, Marty, but can I take just a few more minutes?"

"Of course," Marty responded. He was feeling good about the second C.

Perform as Promised

"Now," Dan continued, moving to the edge of his seat. "We've talked about being consistent in your behaviors, actions, approach, and traditions. We've also talked about how consistency reinforces your clarity and in a lot of ways is your clarity in action." Marty nodded, agreeing with what Dan was saying. "Here are my final few thoughts."

Marty leaned forward again in his chair to show he was still very interested in what Dan was saying.

"Remember, consistency is a lot about creating trust through dependability and reliability even with the simple things. A phrase I like to use to remind me and even others to be consistent is to always perform as promised."

This sounded interesting. Marty continued to listen.

"What I mean by this is that you need to do what you say you're going to do as boss. Like I talked about earlier, if you say, for example, you're going to have a meeting at 9:00 a.m. every Thursday to discuss patient care, then do it. And make sure it happens consistently. Almost nothing is more infuriating than a boss who never follows through with what they say or a boss you can never believe. Don't forget people remember and overanalyze every word you speak. When you say you'll get back to someone in an hour, then you can bet they'll be watching the clock, hoping to hear from you in an hour. Too many leaders lose the trust of their teams as a result of broken promises."

Marty understood. After all, he'd seen leaders who made a lot of promises but never seemed to keep them. His last boss was a perfect example of this, Marty thought. He had promised Marty would have plenty of time to spend with Dan before his last day, and here they were, meeting together at work during Dan's first week of retirement. Marty felt a rush of frustration wash over him but quickly let it go, realizing there wasn't anything he could do about it at this point. In his mind, he knew exactly how aggravating it could be when a boss made promises he didn't keep.

"I think many leaders sometimes aren't careful about what they say, and although they have good intentions to follow up with someone in an hour, for example, they don't really think it through. Again, the people you lead will hold you to your word. They will expect you to do what you say you're going to do. If you fail to deliver, you diminish your influence as a leader. And once trust is lost, it's hard to earn back. So you must be careful in what you say and make sure you always intend to do what you say. You must consistently keep your word."

"I get this," Marty said. Though he wasn't about to share any details, he added, "I've seen this happen and understand how frustrating it can be when a leader does this."

Seeming satisfied, Dan said, "Some of us, we just have to work at this more than others. Again, the point is consistency. It's creating a sense of dependability and assurance that builds trust. When high levels of trust and security exist among your team, it will lead to greater success. That's why when you say you're going to do something, do it. Being inconsistent with what you say or do can become a major disruption to the levels of consistency you'll want to build in order to run a good business and be a great boss."

Marty considered this in his mind, and he knew it was true.

Dan added, "Remember, the key to consistency is discipline."

Marty thought that being consistent by following through with what you say you're going to do again sounded simple in theory but was hard in practice. He determined at that moment he would do his best to have the discipline consistency required. Marty wanted to be consistent. He wanted to be an awesome boss!

Leaving

"I believe it's time for me to go," Dan said as he stood up from his chair stretching. "Now, I know I've mentioned this, but all the *C*'s fit together and build on one another. Hopefully, you can see how consistency and clarity work together and build on each other—how consistency reinforces your clarity."

Marty could see how consistency was a perfect companion to clarity. They certainly fit together in his mind as he reflected on what Dan had taught him. "I think I've got it."

"I hope so, Marty," Dan said. "They're both so important."

Both smiled, and Marty stood and extended his hand. Dan shook it and said, "Well, we've covered a lot today, and I've probably almost made you crazy talking about consistency so much." Dan took a side step toward the door. "As much as I'm enjoying our conversation, I guess it's time for me to leave you alone to think about this. Besides, that phone of yours over there has been lighting up like crazy." He pointed to Marty's cell phone on the far edge of his desk.

Whether that was true or not, Marty wasn't sure. With his phone on silent, he hadn't paid much attention to it.

Dan added, "I know you have a lot to do, and I don't want to keep you any longer than I need to. Besides, I'd hate for you to use me as an excuse for why you can't get anything done around here."

Dan smiled widely, and Marty let out a "Ha! That might not be a bad idea. Do you think that excuse will work?"

Both smiled. As the two walked toward the door, Marty added with sincerity, "Thank you, Dan, for your time today. I really appreciate it."

And with that, Dan was out the door.

***

The rest of Marty's day was a whirlwind. As soon as Dan left, Kate bombarded him with a list of people who had called or stopped by to see him. Then there was something about the fire alarm not working, followed by a code blue on the second floor. Marty then skillfully worked through a few problems that afternoon and even had a good first meeting with Dr. Simpson. Although Marty's day was much busier than he would have liked, such was the nature of the business and his new position. And because things were so busy, he had little time to think too much more about what he and Dan had talked about earlier in the day.

On his late ride home that night he thought about consistency and how it could help him be a great boss. There was no doubt in his mind at this point that focusing on consistency would help him be a better leader for his team and a better person for his family. Though he was exhausted after a long day and couldn't wait for his head to hit the pillow, he felt a little thrill of anticipation for the morning when he'd discover the third *C* in the model to leadership success.

Part Three

Celebration

The Third *C*

It was a new day. Although there appeared to be cloudy weather outside his office window this fall morning, it didn't match Marty's mood. Despite the fact he got little sleep again last night with the first two *C*'s racing through his mind, he still felt eager to meet with Dan and continue their discussion on the four *C*'s model. He knew this was a rare opportunity to be tutored so closely by one of the most successful leaders in the company's history. He felt he needed to do all he could to take advantage of it. Marty's main worry this morning was how quickly he'd be able to implement all four *C*'s at his center. He didn't want to wait—he wanted to make a good first impression and have an immediate positive impact on his team as the new CEO. He knew, though, that he was impatient by nature, so he tried to remind himself often that it took Dan many years to master them. He also realized he still had a lot to learn.

Scanning his office, Marty decided it was time to put out some of his personal belongings. He had been so busy the last two days that he hadn't had time to do much for his office, and it felt pretty empty in the quietness of the morning.

While Marty was still carefully setting out a few of his things, Dan practically burst through the door with a booming "Good morning," then flashed a smile. If Marty had been feeling tired in any way, Dan would have chased it away with his grand entrance. Marty smiled back, surprised by his antics and wondering what he was up to.

"Sorry if I startled you, Marty. I just couldn't help it. It felt too strange yesterday knocking, so I thought today I'd act like I owned the place," Dan said as his eyes squinted, and he chuckled. Before Marty could get in a word, Dan said with real enthusiasm, "Well, we are on our third *C*. Are you ready to celebrate?" He walked swiftly toward Marty and plopped down in his usual chair across the desk.

Marty was already enjoying Dan's energy this morning and really couldn't wait to find out what the next *C* was. "You know, there's an obvious answer to that question," he said, trying to match Dan's enthusiasm without much success. He waited for a moment to build some dramatic effect before saying, "Of course I am!"

"Excellent!" Dan said, calming down a bit now. "So let me ask you some questions. How much fun do you like to have at work?"

Marty wondered what Dan was up to, and he hesitated to respond. He finally raised one of his eyebrows, replying, "Fun?"

"That's right, Marty. How much *fun*?" Dan said this again with a little more oomph coming back to his voice. This was a different Dan than Marty had seen over the previous two days.

"Well," Marty said slowly, not sure where the conversation was headed. "I guess I haven't really ever thought about it. I guess I would say I'd like to have a lot of fun at work, but I also realize it probably isn't something that could ever really happen."

Dan looked thoughtful before stating, "OK, fair enough, though I may question what you just said later. But for now, how much fun do you think the people who now work for you would like to have at work?"

Again, Marty felt completely perplexed by where the conversation was headed. "I guess most people would probably say they'd like to have a lot of fun at work if they could, but I think most people realize the impracticality of that unless they work at Disneyland or something. I think most people expect that work is work and not really a place for fun."

Dan put his hand to his chin. Nodding slowly, he said, "You know what? I think you just nailed it on the head."

Marty shook his head slightly as he wasn't following. He wondered if somehow he had misunderstood him.

"I think most people would love to work somewhere where they had a lot of fun, but most don't ever expect that. Why would they expect it anyway?" He trailed off as he turned and looked away from Marty.

Marty waited for Dan to continue, but he didn't. Instead, he seemed to be looking at the new picture Marty had just hung on his office wall of a beautiful fairway at a pristine golf course somewhere tropical, perhaps Hawaii. "OK, so what does that have to do with the third *C*?" Marty finally asked, breaking the silence as Dan continued to gaze at the picture.

"Do you like golf?" Dan asked, seemingly changing the subject.

"Yes," Marty answered, chuckling at Dan's evasive answer. "What gave it away?"

Dan ignored Marty's question and asked, "How much?"

"A lot, actually. I'm sorry to admit this, but I spend most of my weekends and vacation time golfing. Do you like golf?" Marty asked, still very confused by their current conversation.

"Actually, I do. But I haven't always had a lot of time to enjoy it. It looks like that's all going to change for me now, if I can ever get myself out of this office," Dan replied, turning his head back to Marty with a smile. "I actually think golfing is a lot of fun, and that's it, Marty. Or at least that's part of it. It's an important part of the third *C*."

Marty was very confused at this point. How was fun or golf a part of the third *C*? He felt lost. He knew neither of these words started with the letter *C*. Though he thought about sarcastically pointing that out, he decided it probably wasn't the best thing to say, so he simply waited for Dan to share more.

Marty noticed that Dan recognized the confused look on his face, and he began to chuckle again, slowly shaking his head. "I guess you're wondering what the third *C* is, aren't you? Well, Marty, I already told you."

Marty was completely lost now. Again, he thought Dan must be referring to fun or golf in some way, but he couldn't come up with a *C* word that meant "fun" or "golf."

He could tell Dan was having fun introducing the third *C* in a very cryptic and roundabout way. Under most circumstances this would have irritated Marty, but Dan was just so full of energy and excitement today that it didn't bother him. In fact, he was actually enjoying it. He laughed to himself. "You're going to have to tell me, because I'm confused. I hope that isn't the third *C*," he added, still chuckling.

Dan laughed. "No, no, it's not. 'Confused' is not the third *C*." Finally feeling like he was being let off the hook, Dan said, "The third *C* is 'celebration.'"

Before Marty could fully grasp what Dan had just said, Dan did something totally unexpected. He stood up from his chair and sang, "Celebrate good times, come on," while raising his hands above his head as if he were attempting some dance move. Marty had to laugh again. He hadn't seen this side of Dan to this point, for sure, and he thought that maybe the freedom and stress-free life of retirement was starting to sink in for him.

"Marty, the third *C* is 'celebration.' You have to enjoy work and make it enjoyable for your team members, and the best way to do that is to celebrate. The more you celebrate, the better off you'll be." Dan walked over to the whiteboard and added to what he had already written. This is what it now looked like:

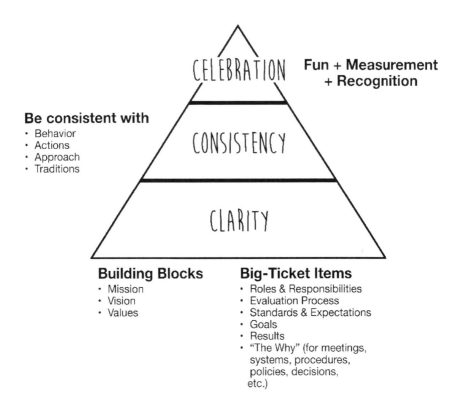

CELEBRATION — **Fun + Measurement + Recognition**

Be consistent with
- Behavior
- Actions
- Approach
- Traditions

CONSISTENCY

CLARITY

Building Blocks
- Mission
- Vision
- Values

Big-Ticket Items
- Roles & Responsibilities
- Evaluation Process
- Standards & Expectations
- Goals
- Results
- "The Why" (for meetings, systems, procedures, policies, decisions, etc.)

"There are three parts to celebration, which I have written on the board," Dan said as he walked back to the chair and plopped down in his seat.

Marty thought about the word *celebration* and how exactly it fit in at work. Dan continued. "How would you feel if the first time you hit your budget goals here in your new position, the COO of Wiser Care took you out golfing to celebrate your success?"

Marty didn't have to think long before responding, "That would be pretty amazing. I'd love it!"

"Do you think that would help make him a better boss? At least in your eyes?" Dan asked, raising his eyebrows as if to add effect.

Again, Marty didn't hesitate. "That would definitely make him an incredible boss in my mind."

Marty instantly began thinking, *Would someone actually do that?* No boss had ever done anything remotely like that for him in the past as an immediate response to his good performance. At least not that he could recall, and he was certain if they had, he'd have remembered it.

"Now, that may be a bit of an unlikely example. I don't mean to get your hopes up, but the point is people like to celebrate and have fun. And why shouldn't they when they're producing good results?"

Marty thought about it, and what Dan had just said did make sense to him.

"As a boss you have a responsibility to help your team feel successful. You can do that by helping them celebrate when they accomplish goals and have great results. It doesn't have to be a fabulous trip to a nice golf course; it can actually be much simpler than that. The most important thing is that you recognize and celebrate good performance."

Marty felt he was beginning to see why celebration fit in the model as the third *C. Everyone likes to be recognized and acknowledged for their results,* he thought.

"You said earlier that most people would like to have fun at work but would never expect it. Why do you think that is?"

Marty had to stop and think about this for a few moments. Finally, he said, "Well, I guess because most work just isn't seen as being that much fun."

"OK, I guess I can buy that in some ways," Dan said slowly. "But there has to be an even better reason. Why do people not expect to have fun at work? I'm serious."

Marty could tell Dan really wanted him to think this through. He was struggling to find a good answer. Finally, the only thing he could come up with came out of his mouth. "Maybe it's because they've never experienced fun at work before."

Dan moved his hand back to his chin as if he were contemplating Marty's answer. "Hmm. I think you may be on to something, Marty. Perhaps people don't expect it because they've never experienced it. I actually really like that." Dan leaned back in his chair and placed his hands behind his head. "I've never considered that, but I think you're probably right.

"How many hours do you spend at work? On average, let's say in a week."

Marty thought about this and worried a little bit again about how to answer. The reality was he was someone who liked to get to work early and even stay late. He took pride in his ability to outwork his colleagues and peers, although he knew it sometimes rubbed people the wrong way. Marty believed that putting in extra time would pay off, and to this point, in his mind, it had.

"I guess about sixty hours a week at the office, maybe a little more." Marty felt he was being a little conservative, but he also didn't want to sound like he was exaggerating. He wondered why he worried about this stuff with Dan. He sincerely felt Dan wasn't someone who needed to be impressed.

"That's a lot, Marty," Dan replied. Marty felt some relief at his answer. "So you put in sixty hours each week at the center and have no fun during this time; is that correct?"

Marty hesitated but again decided he could answer only truthfully. "Well, yes, for the most part. I mean, I enjoy what I do and interacting with staff and people, but—"

Dan cut him off and asked genuinely, "Why? Why do you put in all those hours without any fun? That seems pretty awful."

Marty realized Dan had a point. If he was honest, he had to admit it was awful at times. He often sacrificed things he enjoyed outside of work like his family and even golf to put in long hours. He knew that wasn't unusual, but he thought more about Dan's point.

Suddenly, Marty noticed Dan was waiting for an answer, so he quickly said, "It's not always the easiest thing to do, but I'm committed to our company and really don't mind."

"That is admirable," Dan said sincerely. "Most people won't put in those kinds of hours to get the job done. Wiser Care is lucky to have you."

Marty felt the same sense of pride he always felt when someone recognized him for all the long hours he put in at work. But just as he was feeling good about himself, Dan interrupted his thoughts with another surprising question.

"How much time do you think you might put in if you were having fun while doing it?"

Now this was something that Marty had never considered. He felt he was pretty maxed out with his time and wasn't sure how to answer. He decided he could be honest with Dan. "I guess maybe a little more, but I feel pretty maxed out with my time."

Dan gave Marty what he thought was a reassuring look before saying, "Let me ask it a better way. If you were really enjoying work, and there was an element of fun you could consistently count on, do you think your time spent at work would be more productive? Do you think you might even be able to do more in less time because it seemed more enjoyable?"

Marty had never considered such a possibility. If work was more fun day to day, could he actually get more done in less time? He honestly wasn't sure. "I'm not sure," he replied, realizing that if work was truly fun, he probably would want to be there more often, or at least he'd look forward to being there more than he had in the past.

Marty was about to add to his response when Dan said, "My guess is you probably could. We need to change our whole mind-set about work. We need to change the expectation from 'no fun' to 'lots of fun.' We ask people to spend at least forty hours a week here, and like you, many spend even more than that. Instead of having the expectation that work is not a place to have fun, what if people thought it was a place where they *could* have fun? We can do that when we celebrate often. Work can be fun, Marty. In fact, I think it should be fun.

"I'm not sure how we change the belief in our society that work is not a place for fun. I think it should be the exact opposite. Work can and should be so much fun. When we celebrate success, when we recognize people, when we consistently measure our results and provide a scoreboard to track progress, it is fun. When you do these things, your people will enjoy being here. They may even look forward to coming in each day. And they may even invite their friends and acquaintances to join them."

"Interesting," Marty said quietly. What Dan had said about the third *C* struck a chord with him as thoughts raced through his mind. If he could create an environment where work was truly enjoyable, he was sure two of his potentially biggest worries about his new position would be minimized. Though Marty hadn't admitted it to anyone, ever since the invitation to become a CEO had come, he had been really anxious about two problems nearly every one of his previous bosses had always complained about openly and struggled with deeply: employee turnover and recruiting new staff.

Health care was hitting a crisis point with nursing shortages, and the ability to find and retain staff had caused a lot of problems at so many of the centers he had worked at. He knew that in order to be successful, he'd need to find good staff, but he worried about how to do that. Creating a place where people actually sensed a real element of fun, where the team celebrated success and liked being together, sounded to Marty like something that could be really effective. Though an unexpected answer that might not completely eliminate these problems, he could see how creating this kind of work environment could really help. Besides, Dan had often led the organization in employee satisfaction results, not to mention his consistency in holding one of the best employee turnover rates at his center. Maybe the four C's were the real solution to these huge problems. Marty was quickly warming up to the idea of the third C and the implications of following through with it.

The four C's model may be more valuable than I ever imagined, Marty thought. He noticed Dan's enthusiasm must have rubbed off on him as he felt a tremendous sense of excitement learning about the third C.

Celebrations

After a quick break in the conversation to grab some water bottles, the two colleagues sat back in their usual places across from each other. Marty was eager to hear more about celebration when Dan continued. "Celebrations bring us together as human beings and help us connect and build strong relationships. Think about it. Outside work, how often do we celebrate? We have holidays, birthdays, anniversaries, graduations, big games, christenings, and many other special events and occasions that cause us to celebrate. I bet some of your most cherished memories are centered on celebrating something with someone. I also bet the things you look forward to most are upcoming celebrations with your family and friends."

Marty thought about what Dan had shared, and he certainly thought he had a point. As he contemplated it more, Marty recalled a few months ago when he and his wife, April, celebrated their ten-year wedding anniversary. They took a very nice trip to the West Coast to celebrate. It was something they planned together and then looked forward to for a long time. Hiking in the Redwood National and State Parks with his bride was something he would not soon forget. It was an incredible trip and a fun way to celebrate their anniversary.

Marty decided he had to admit Dan definitely had a point. Celebrating was an important part of his life, and many of his fondest memories did center around a celebration of some sort.

Dan interrupted Marty's thoughts with a question. "So why not celebrate often at work?"

Marty had time to think about it for only a moment when Dan added, "If celebrations are absent from our workplace, we're missing out on a tremendous opportunity to strengthen the relationships among our team members. We're missing a chance to create happy and lasting memories at work. We are missing out on events that people who work for us can look forward to."

"I think I see your point," Marty responded. The truth was thoughts were now swirling around in his mind. He contemplated how having celebrations at work could bring people together just as they did outside work. "I can honestly say I've never considered something like this before. I think this may just work," Marty said the last part almost more to himself than to Dan.

Marty paused for a few more seconds and asked, "Can you maybe give me some more examples of how you've celebrated with your team?"

"I thought you'd never ask," Dan said with a smile.

"One of the best celebrations we had in our center recently was when we hit a big financial goal we'd been striving for. We didn't do anything extravagant, but we had a great time together. We celebrated by having a *Minute to Win It* competition among our team members. It probably lasted only thirty minutes or so and cost us a few rolls of toilet paper, some ping-pong balls, some disposable plastic cups, some cookies, and some Kleenex boxes. Oh, and of course good snacks with green punch." Dan said this with a wink. "And a few fun prizes for the winners. A few of us put it together in no time at all, and it was a ton of fun. Our team is still talking about it."

Marty thought about how easy Dan made it sound. *Perhaps it is easy*, Marty thought.

"And that celebration is a memory we'll share together for a lifetime." Chuckling now, he said, "Trust me, no one will ever forget how ridiculous I looked as I tripped over my feet while being wrapped in toilet paper by my VP of clinical services and VP of marketing. We were so close to beating that team of nurses until I decided to fall." Dan snapped his fingers, still chuckling. "This is an example of what I'm talking about. It's an example of celebration."

Marty really liked the sound of it. He did still have a concern, though, and he knew it was time to bring it up.

The Celebration Question

"Now I don't want to dampen the mood," Marty said, easing into his concern, "but is it possible to celebrate and at the same time get all the work done? I worry that celebration might distract people from the seriousness of our work."

Dan quickly responded to the question as if he had already anticipated it was coming. "Remember, Marty, there's more to the third *C*. Fun is only part of it. Celebration does help invite fun into the workplace, which is so important, but that isn't all of it. Celebration is also about measurement and recognition. Sure, you can celebrate just to celebrate, like on people's birthdays or work anniversaries or holidays, or even just for the fun of it, but if that's all you do, it simply isn't enough. You need to find ways to celebrate more. You need to celebrate when goals are reached and even when progress is being made."

Marty wasn't sure what to think. On the one hand, he liked the idea of celebrations being tied to results, but on the other hand, he was still conflicted because Dan was talking about even more celebrations. *Maybe he didn't understand my question*, Marty thought.

"Marty, the best leaders set clear goals, standards, and values for their team, and when the team achieves those goals, upholds the standards, or lives the values they celebrate. If you fail to do this when good things are happening around here, people may begin to feel their work and efforts are unnoticed or that they aren't all that important to you."

Marty leaned back in his chair now, trying to take in all Dan was sharing.

"And coming back to fun, if you can't have fun and relax together every once in a while, it will be hard to reach your full potential as a team. Celebration gives people a chance to connect and engage in a totally different way. It connects and binds people together at a whole new level—a level that would not be achievable otherwise. For these reasons, good leaders help their people celebrate." Dan said this with some extra conviction in his voice.

Marty believed Dan was making some good points, but he still worried people might only want to have fun and not get any real work done. *What am I missing?*, he thought.

"So, you brought up some really good questions a few minutes ago. These are questions almost every leader has when learning this part of the model, and they are very valid. Before we completely answer them together, let me ask you a question."

"Sure, go ahead," Marty said, feeling relief that there was still more.

"Has there ever been a time when you've celebrated something you accomplished at work?"

Marty thought about it for a second. "Well, a team I was working with a few years ago developed a customer service initiative that led to the highest customer satisfaction scores in our company. In fact, based on the responses we received, our customers were so satisfied at the center where we implemented the program that we even gained some national recognition for our scores."

"Oh yes, I remember that. You were part of that group?" Dan sounded genuinely excited. "That was legendary for our company! The customer service program you helped create was truly remarkable," he added enthusiastically. "We implemented here much of what you did at that center when we learned about it. It's helped us out a lot, just brilliant."

"Thank you," Marty said proudly. He was excited that Dan not only knew about the program but also had implemented some of it in his center. "Sandy, the CEO of Wiser Care, as you know, was so excited with our success that she personally invited each one of us who was part of that team to a formal dinner at the corporate offices after hours. I wasn't sure what to expect. When we arrived, I was shocked. The corporate office had been transformed into an elegant restaurant. It really was quite amazing. Each of us was able to invite a guest to join us, and they served the best food. There was also some live entertainment, waiters, a dance-off..." Marty smiled. "It was really a wonderful evening with Sandy and her spouse right there at the corporate office. It was a special experience, one I'll never forget, and one my wife still talks about. She had such a great time there too."

Marty sat thinking about that evening and added, "Since then, during some of my darkest days at Wiser Care, I still think back on that particular night and how Sandy recognized our team for our hard work and accomplishments. Those memories have always offered me the motivation I've needed to continue working through the hard times."

Dan said, "Sounds like quite the celebration. I'm jealous I missed it."

Marty continued. "Each time I think about that memory, it motivates me to want to try harder to develop similar results so that I can perhaps have another great experience like that one."

"Thanks for sharing that with me. And that does sound like something Sandy would do. I guess you could say her celebrations are a little more sophisticated than mine are here," Dan said with a big grin. "I can only imagine how that evening made you feel."

Marty agreed that he and his colleagues felt extremely appreciated that evening for all their hard work and sacrifices to complete the project. That memory truly did motivate Marty every time he thought about the experience. In fact, those who attended the event were the people Marty still felt most connected to in the organization. They had a special bond because of that evening together. And the fact that his wife was invited to enjoy it with him was the cherry on top. It helped her see the value his work was creating and the good his company was doing. It even made her push him a little more, and she seemed more understanding when he was wrapped up in his work or arrived home later than expected. And then all of a sudden, it hit him. The third *C* had indeed been invaluable to him personally.

"So, do you think this celebration affected you negatively or kept you from the work you needed to get done? Did it take away from the seriousness of your work?" Dan questioned.

Snapping back from the epiphany he had just experienced, Marty replied, "No. If anything, it did just the opposite. It motivated me to want to have similar if not better results the next time. It motivated me to be better and try harder. It made me feel appreciated and important. And I can think of no other time in my career when I've had more fun at work than with that team. We did so much together and had a good time doing it, and then we celebrated."

"That's great," Dan said, and Marty could tell he was a little surprised by his response. "Can you honestly think of any celebration that you've participated in at work that made you want to work less or not take work seriously?"

As Marty thought about it, he knew he probably had the answer already. He did want to think about it, though. After a few moments, he realized he couldn't think of any. The truth was, the more he thought about it, the more he realized even the small celebrations he remembered made him want to try harder and do better. Like the time his first manager had handed out a pack of gum to everyone after a really hard day. Despite the late night, his boss had taken time not just to purchase the gum, but each pack included a note that said, "Sticking together like a team always should—thank you!" It was such a small gesture, but it meant something to Marty.

Or the day his coworkers completely surprised him with a birthday cake and balloons. He was not expecting that at all, and it felt nice to know they cared. Or even the time his previous boss decided to serve ice cream in the lobby of their health care center because they had reached a goal, and he wanted everyone to know it. The team loved that simple act of celebration, and Marty enjoyed taking a turn serving ice cream to them. In the end, each of these celebrations, whether big or small, brought good feelings and positive memories to Marty. Even when the celebrations were cheesy or Marty didn't find them particularly interesting, he still always appreciated the thought and the recognition. Marty did have to admit that the celebrations he remembered most were the exact things that motivated him to stay with Wiser Care and to try just a little harder.

"You got me," Marty said. "I can't really think of a celebration at work that has negatively affected my work or made me take it less seriously."

Dan seemed to be pushing Marty a little more now, asking, "What would have happened if you and your team had received these great results for your customer satisfaction initiative, yet no one at work said anything about it to you? What if there was no celebration at all? What if Sandy and the rest of the corporate office never even said a word?" Dan shrugged his shoulders.

Marty didn't need to think too much about that one. "I know I would have still been proud of our team. But I can say I wouldn't feel as motivated to do it again, nor would I feel the same level of respect and appreciation I have now for Sandy." He thought a little bit more and added, "I probably wouldn't feel as valued as a leader in our organization, either. I might have even wondered if the company really cared all that much about the success of the initiative. And…" Marty paused for a moment, thinking before saying, "I would have missed out on a memorable experience that I now share with many of my colleagues in the organization, including the CEO."

"Well said," Dan responded as he leaned back in his chair, looking satisfied.

Marty sat thinking for a few moments and then said, "It sounds like celebration is even more than what I have experienced, though. These celebrations I've thought about haven't happened every day. In fact, they've been pretty rare. But it sounds like you're saying celebrations need to happen more often."

Dan smiled but didn't say anything. Marty was trying to decide what he might be thinking.

After stretching for a minute, Dan moved forward in his chair and said, "If you remember, celebration is more than just having fun. It's also about measurement. What that means is if the team isn't getting results, and if you aren't making progress, then celebrations probably won't be as big as they could be. At least they won't be on the scale of what you might have if you were reaching them."

That certainly seemed logical to Marty. Dan added, "Setting goals with your team and then measuring progress toward them gives you reasons to celebrate. It gives you a scoreboard of sorts. If you don't set goals, or if you do set goals but you never track your progress toward reaching them, you'll miss way too many opportunities to celebrate. Setting goals and then measuring them consistently is very important to establishing the third *C*."

Marty felt like he was slowly grasping all that celebration was about, and it really did make him excited. He waited to see if Dan would go on. As if reading his mind, Dan continued.

"Sure, it's fun and important to celebrate birthdays and holidays and other special occasions, but what really adds power to this *C* is when celebrations are tied to performance. Like the 'Minute to Win It' party I talked about. We didn't randomly celebrate just to have fun, though that would be OK to do," Dan said with a wink, "but we celebrated to recognize an achievement of a goal we had reached as a team. And at our center here, the bigger the goals reached, often the bigger the celebration."

Dan sat up straight and added, "Like your evening with Sandy. That was a big celebration to recognize your team's big achievement. I know it took years developing, testing, and then fully implementing that program. It was a big deal. The celebration you had with Sandy was tied to the achievement."

Marty nodded in agreement.

"Without goals and tracking progress toward them, you probably won't celebrate enough, and you probably won't recognize the progress the team is making. In fact, without clarity and measurement around goals, it will be hard to know when to celebrate."

Marty liked the sound of that. He could see how clarity and celebration worked together. He picked up his notepad and wrote "measurement" and "fun" below where he had written the word *celebration*.

"But things won't always go well, and there will not always be big and obvious reasons to celebrate. You may not reach your goals, and results may be bad. As a boss, sometimes you have to get creative because you can't forget this *C* in the good times or the bad. Like the first two *C*'s, you should constantly be striving to establish this *C*. If you want to be as successful as you can be as a leader, you'll look for reasons to celebrate."

Marty looked up, feeling a little in doubt again about his understanding of the third *C*.

"If I understand right, it seems the first two *C*'s, clarity and consistency, are things leaders must do every day, constantly clarifying and being consistent, while celebration is something you worry about every once in a while. Like when a goal is achieved."

Dan smiled. "Not exactly, but nice try."

Marty felt again like he had somehow missed something.

Everyday Celebrations

After a moment, Dan leaned back in his chair, crossed his legs, and relaxed his hands, holding them in his lap. He looked at Marty and said, "I've been so excited about sharing celebration with you that I don't think I've made it very clear."

Marty didn't think Dan had been unclear; he thought just the opposite was true. He had already learned a lot about the value of celebration but obviously needed to learn more. Before he could say anything, Dan went on.

"Just like the first two *C*'s, celebration is something great leaders focus on and strive to establish every single day. Sure, you won't have the big celebrations that we've talked about every day, like your evening with Sandy or my 'Minute to Win It' party. But that doesn't mean you shouldn't be finding simple ways to celebrate daily. Remember, celebration has three parts. It's a combination of fun, measurement, and recognition. You can establish celebration as a boss by recognizing people's good work each day. A thank-you card, a high five, a congratulatory comment, and even a sincere smile are some of the simplest celebrations but can actually be some of the most powerful. These simple daily gestures of celebration communicate to your team that you recognize their good work and efforts. They show you're excited about good results and performance, and they make work more fun."

Marty nodded as the idea of daily celebrations sank in.

"Do you remember when I talked about our daily morning meeting—our morning huddle?"

"Yes," Marty said. He recalled how it had helped Dan improve communication and establish clarity.

"Another reason why I am grateful we started those many years ago is because it gives me another easy way to celebrate. Each day I recognize someone in front of their peers for doing a good job, and often we give each other a round of applause when big tasks or tough challenges are mastered. This is another example of a simple daily celebration."

Marty thought he was finally getting it now.

"You can also even help individual team members celebrate in small ways and help them measure the impact they're having on your business. Do you mind if I share an example with you?"

"Of course," Marty replied, curious about how he could help an individual staff member celebrate.

"A few years ago, our receptionist, Michelle, who sits in the front lobby, was struggling in her role. Answering phones around here is literally a full-time job, and it can get exhausting," Dan added. "Anyway, back in those days, Michelle always seemed to be…" Dan thought for a moment before saying, "Well, always in a bad mood. I'm sure there were a lot of reasons for this, but it was affecting our customer service. I even felt a little uncomfortable being around her because she always seemed either unhappy or upset. And if I felt uncomfortable around her, imagine how our visitors must have felt."

Marty thought it probably was pretty bad. If someone couldn't show better behavior around their CEO, he shuddered to think how she might have been behaving toward others.

"After thinking about the situation, I realized that she had no good way to measure her impact or contribution to our center. So I sat down with her and first explained how important her role was to our center and in helping us live our mission. I knew she needed to hear her job mattered. I tried to connect what she did to what we were trying to accomplish each day. Then we came up with a plan to measure her performance on a daily basis. We decided that good performance for her could be measured by the number of smiles she received from people each day. After all, she was normally the first person people met as they walked through our door."

Marty sat intrigued by where Dan's story was going.

"We set an initial goal of fifty smiles in one day. To be honest, I thought it would be hard for her to reach it, but within a few days, she got it, and we celebrated together with high fives and a 'That Was Easy' button for her desk. She loved that," Dan said with a smile.

"We then set a new goal, and she reached it and then another and then another. This continued for nearly a year as each time she set a new record for the most smiles she received in a day, we celebrated with things such as small prizes, certificates, high fives, praise, recognition in our daily huddle, and a few other fun ways.

"Though I've stopped celebrating with her daily like I did, she still keeps track of the number of smiles she receives each day and often gives me a report. This has been a lot of fun for both of us and helps her stay motivated and focused. It's also helped her recognize the tremendous impact she has on our customers both on the phone and in our front lobby."

Marty was again impressed with how simple yet effective Dan's methods were. Dan then added, "Best of all, she really loves working here. Before, I could tell she wasn't too happy at work."

Marty shook his head slowly, now soaking it all in. The combination of the first three C's seemed to have had an amazing impact on the team. It also seemed that if applied

149

effectively, it could make a leader unstoppable. *And the elements of the model are so simple, yet leaders obviously don't give them enough attention*, Marty thought.

"Oh, and her latest record now is three hundred and eighty-nine smiles in a day."

Marty was surprised.

A Time to Leave

Marty believed he was really starting to understand the importance of celebration, and he could feel Dan's energy toward it. He was hoping Dan would share more, and almost as if on cue, Dan started reflecting back to earlier in their conversation.

"You know, Marty, I'm sure I would have felt the way you described if nothing had been done by Sandy or her team after I worked so hard on that customer service initiative. Like you, my motivation to do it again probably would have been much lower if something like that hadn't happened." Dan leaned forward and put his hands on his knees. "In fact, one of the most challenging bosses I ever worked for was right here in this office. I was new to the company and had been talked into joining it after a friend of mine wouldn't take no for an answer." He smiled. "Before then, I worked with one of our closest competitors." Marty knew Dan had worked somewhere else prior to joining Wiser but had no details. He was interested to learn more.

"All my coworkers at my previous employer thought I was crazy when I decided to leave. I had built up a pretty good reputation over there, and my peers assumed I was on a fast track to promotions and other opportunities." Marty hadn't ever considered what might have happened had Dan not chosen to join Wiser Care. Dan was so ingrained and such an important part of Wiser Care's story that it was hard to envision such a possibility.

"The truth, however, was that I wasn't all that happy working for my former employer for various reasons. When I finally gave in to my friend and agreed to an interview with my then-future boss here at Wiser Care, I was so impressed by him. During the interview he told me about his audacious goals for revenue growth, quality care, innovation, and customer service. He explained he wanted me to be a big part of it all. I was so excited by the vision he laid out in front of me that I nearly asked him when I could start in the middle of our interview."

Marty shifted in his chair, still interested in what Dan was sharing, though he began to wonder what this story might have to do with celebration. Rather than interrupting, he slowly nodded to show he was listening.

"Later, when I started here, I met a wonderful coworker named Paul who had started a few weeks before me. Paul and I hit it off immediately because we..." Dan hesitated for a moment as if trying to find the right words. "We were both young and hungry. We both wanted to make our new boss's vision a reality. We both wanted to be the best, and we wanted to work for the best. We talked about this often together and pushed each other. We became quite the pair."

Marty thought about what it might be like to have two Dans at one center. *It must have been really nice for his boss*, he thought to himself.

Dan continued. "Paul and I began to work tirelessly along with many others on the team to not only achieve but also exceed the monthly goals set out for us. To make a long story short, we actually did it. And we did it much faster than we ever anticipated. Paul and I were so excited, but our excitement didn't last very long."

Marty raised his eyebrows, and Dan continued. "The reason is that nothing was ever said about our success. We waited and waited but didn't hear from anyone at all—and our boss acted like it was no big deal. Soon he let us know that our monthly goals had been changed and that we needed to stretch higher and improve things even more. Our boss acted as if the original goals we met were insignificant and no big deal, almost making it feel like we were falling short of expected performance. Yet if I remember right, we had just achieved results the center had never seen to that point."

Marty was surprised. From the sound of it, Dan and his colleagues had done some pretty remarkable things, so why wouldn't his boss or even someone else at Wiser Care make a bigger deal of it? He realized he was beginning to feel frustrated just listening to Dan's story. He thought perhaps it was partly because he had grown to really like Dan and felt he deserved a great deal of recognition, and perhaps it was partly because, though not as extreme, he had experienced similar situations during his career.

"I wouldn't say I expected a whole lot from my boss or even anyone else, but literally nothing was ever said. In our minds we believed we had just accomplished something great."

Dan sat as if he were reminiscing about that moment in time, then added, "Perhaps as young professionals, we were overinflating our achievements."

Marty was still surprised by the lack of acknowledgment from Dan's boss.

"Anyway," Dan continued, "I started to wonder if our success was really success at all because of the lack of celebration or recognition. As much as I tried to fight it, I also began to wonder if I had made a mistake by leaving my old employer. At least over there people recognized I was doing a good job. It seemed to me at that time that no one really cared much about my results at Wiser and that no matter what I achieved, the bar would always be placed higher out of reach. I began to realize our results would never be recognized or seen as good enough. I worried I'd never be able to advance in my career, which was my goal. It was a really bad feeling."

Finally, Marty felt compelled to speak up. "I can't believe your boss didn't recognize you and your team for all that you had done," he said with a little bit more frustration than he wanted to show.

Thankfully, Dan went on.

"Paul and I soon became discouraged by the reality we were living in. We both were so competitive and wanted to be acknowledged. We wanted to advance our careers, but if no one recognized our efforts, we didn't see a path that made it possible at Wiser Care." Dan sort of smiled but put his head down, shaking it slowly. Marty could tell this incident, which must have occurred nearly thirty years ago, still had a powerful effect on Dan as he relived it. Marty was curious how he'd pulled through it.

"I remember my enthusiasm for achieving results was waning, and this bothered me because I always believed I was a self-motivated person and didn't necessarily need recognition from others. And unlike you, at this time, I hadn't had any great experiences with the company or the CEO of Wiser Care to fall back on. So, I decided to leave the company."

Marty's jaw nearly hit the floor, and he held back the urge to shout, *What?* Internally, when people spoke about Wiser Care, they spoke about Dan Rosier. He was known and respected by literally every leader in the organization. His reputation was legendary. Never had Marty imagined that Dan had left the company at one time.

"You left the company?" Marty blurted out. "I never knew that!"

"Yep," Dan said, laughing uncomfortably. "I left. I went back to my previous employer and didn't return for just over three years. When I was finally convinced to come back, the boss I'd had at Wiser Care had left the company. And to be honest, I didn't have to be convinced to come back. I actually begged."

Just when he didn't think it was possible, Marty's interest in learning more about Dan's story grew. He never imagined that Dan had done anything "wrong" at Wiser Care because of his near-impeccable reputation around the company, yet he had learned so many surprising things about Dan's journey. Marty was dying to know more about what happened. Rather than say something silly, he took a drink of water from a bottle on the corner of his desk and tried to calm himself down before he spoke.

"I know it's surprising," Dan said with a slight grin. "I left the company, Marty, but I couldn't come back soon enough. Let me tell you why."

"Please do" was all Marty could say as he put down his bottle of water and sat on the edge of his chair, ready to listen to the rest of the story.

"That CEO you were talking about earlier personally invited me out to dinner one night. At the time, I wasn't exactly sure why she had invited me. I had only briefly met her once. Sandy joined the company as a young VP a little bit before I left."

Marty decided it was time to show he had relaxed a little, and he made an attempt to tease Dan. "That must have been a loooong time ago." He drew out the word *long* and opened his eyes wide.

Dan smiled. "Trust me. My knees agree with you that it was a long time ago." Both of them smiled for a moment, and then Dan continued.

"When I arrived at dinner still wondering what this invitation was about, she thanked me for all the success Paul and I had when I had worked for Wiser Care previously. She said when she joined the company, she recognized quickly the incredible growth we at our health care center were having, and she wanted to personally thank me for all that we had done. When I heard this, I probably looked even more stunned than you looked a few minutes ago." Dan laughed. "After over three years, I still held some resentment for never having received any recognition for our efforts, and for all I knew, no one had even noticed or cared. Yet here was this important person from another company inviting me to dinner and thanking me personally for achievements that had happened a long time ago. During that evening, she never said anything to me about coming back to Wiser Care, but you can believe me when I say I stayed up all night wanting to come back. In fact, I begged to come back after that night because I was still not satisfied with my previous employer. And Sandy had renewed my belief in Wiser Care."

"Wow," Marty said quietly, thinking about the implications of not utilizing the third C, of not celebrating success. "I can see why celebration is so important. I see how, without it, those you lead may feel they are not valued, appreciated, and recognized."

"It's true," Dan said.

Dan looked like he was contemplating something. "Now, I know this story was more about our company here, but as I've gotten older and wiser, I've realized the biggest reason I was never very happy with my other employer was because of the absence of the four C's."

Marty thought about that. He was amazed by the impact the four C's could have on someone as successful and respected as Dan. He realized that life without them would make work pretty miserable. Dan's story also reminded Marty again how critical his new role was and how big of an impact he'd have on others' lives.

Celebration Wrap-Up

Dan interrupted Marty's thoughts. "Marty, remember, celebration is more than just fun, measurement or, recognition in isolation. If that was the case, then one of those words would be at the top of the pyramid over there." Dan pointed to the whiteboard. "Celebration is the right word for the model because it's a word that incorporates and includes all three of those things. Without some element of fun, measurement, or recognition, you're missing the mark with celebration. And celebration is most powerful when it emphasizes results. Celebrations at work, just as in life, help create positive lasting memories."

Marty soaked all this in. He felt like he now had a good idea of what celebration was and how it fit into the model. It seemed appropriate that it was the top of the pyramid. *The icing on the cake*, he thought.

Marty was so excited about the first three C's, he felt he could hardly wait for the last. More than ever, he was tempted to ask Dan to stay longer and persuade him to share the last C. Before he mustered the courage to ask, Dan said, "Remember, having celebrations together builds stronger relationships. They help foster teamwork and trust. Consistency with celebrations can create an incredible environment where memorable experiences bind people together and make them feel committed to one another. Think about how your evening with Sandy did that for you and your coworkers."

Dan was right. Marty also felt a little sorry he had doubted the third *C*, even if it had been just for a brief moment. Based on all Dan had shared with him, Marty saw the powerful impact celebration could have on his team.

Dan said, "Also remember that celebration, just like the other *C*'s in the model, is something you need to strive to establish every day. You should be finding simple ways to celebrate with your team members daily. In fact, the key to celebration is frequency."

Dan seemed to relax now, as if he might be finished. Marty looked over at the board where Dan had written the model, and in a flash, something hit him.

"Wait, the pyramid is complete," he said, feeling concerned. He looked back at the whiteboard to double-check. "I thought you said there were four *C*'s, but there's no more room in the pyramid."

"Ah, good catch," Dan said with a smile, as if he was glad Marty had brought it up. "Don't worry, Marty. There is a forth *C*, but it isn't part of the pyramid. It plays a different role in the model than the others. In some ways, it's the most influential of all the *C*'s. I'll explain more how the fourth *C* works tomorrow."

Marty tried to hide his disappointment. He really wanted to learn more now. Having to wait each day for the next *C* was torturous. In the end, he decided he needed to be patient. He didn't want Dan to rush through the next *C*, and he certainly didn't want him to not come back tomorrow. Marty knew that though he was eager to learn more, it would be best to wait.

"You like to keep me in suspense, don't you?" Marty asked with a mischievous smile.

Dan also smiled. "The fourth *C* really is important and deserves our full attention. I'll allow you to think about celebration this afternoon and evening, and then let's begin again first thing in the morning on the fourth *C* to leadership success." Marty could tell Dan could detect what he was thinking and smiled to himself.

"Sounds like a great plan," Marty said reassuringly.

The two leaders shook hands before Dan headed out the office door.

***

The rest of Wednesday proved to be just as busy and just as intense as the last two days. Marty wondered if it would let up soon as he headed home late again that evening. He was accustomed to the long days and all the demands of a health care center, but now, as the CEO, the heavy load seemed to be much greater. Despite the busyness of the day, Marty did think about how he could celebrate with his team. Though he had always strived to recognize his people and show them appreciation, he knew celebration was more than what he had done in the past.

As these thoughts churned around in his head, Marty decided he needed to stop and surprise his wife with a little celebration of their own. After all, she had put up with these long hours for a long time, and it was likely going to only get worse before it got better. Marty's wife loved chocolate cheesecake, and when he walked through the door holding it out with some flowers in his other hand, she squealed. Marty enjoyed his night talking about the three *C*'s and celebrating with his wife.

160

Part Four

Charity

The Multiplier

As Marty rolled down the interstate heading in to work Thursday morning, his head was filled with thoughts and ideas about the three *C's* he had learned thus far. Though he was excited about what he had learned, he also recognized he was growing more nervous about following in the footsteps of someone who seemed so proficient at implementing them. If anything, Marty decided, this should encourage him to be even more committed to them. Marty knew this type of challenge would be good for him. He also realized his highly successful team would be disappointed if their new leader didn't strive to implement the *C's*—he was sure they had grown accustomed to working for a leader who lived by them. He also was certain they would gladly help if he asked them to. And this was something he planned to do soon, but for now, he wanted to wait until he knew the entire model.

As he walked passed Kate's empty desk and through his office door, Marty recognized his enthusiasm for day four was slightly lower than for the previous days. Part of it was because he was tired. A bigger part however was that although he wanted to learn the fourth *C*, he also reflected on the fact that this was most likely his last chance to spend quality time with Dan. This thought gave him a feeling of sadness and disappointment. He really wished he could continue his morning conversations with Dan a little while longer, even if they were putting him behind at work.

As he placed his briefcase on the large desk and opened his blind to let the morning sunlight pour in, the thought that this was not only his last day with Dan but also probably Dan's last day to spend significant time helping Wiser Care didn't sit right with him. He wondered if there wasn't more the company could do to keep Dan around a little bit longer, even on a part-time basis. Dan was such an integral part of Wiser Care's success over the years—after all, he had led the top center for two decades. At that moment Marty decided he'd let Sandy know about all Dan had taught him. He wanted to suggest the company do more to see if Dan would stick around to teach it to all the CEOs. *After all, Dan is younger than most people who retire; at least he sure seems like it*, Marty thought. Marty also wondered if Sandy knew about the four C's model and if she would be open to trying to apply it more fully across the entire organization. Knowing Sandy, Marty felt certain she would once she learned about it.

As Marty turned on his laptop and sat contemplating this quietly in his office, Dan opened the door, not as animated as the day before but still with a big smile on his face and the same level of energy that always seemed to defy his age. He practically skipped over to the desk and stuck out his hand. Marty stood, smiled, and shook it. "Well," Dan said, still smiling, "did you get a chance to celebrate last night, knowing this will be one of your last days with me?"

"Just the opposite," Marty said with emphasis. Though Marty had celebrated last night with his wife, it wasn't because his time with Dan was coming to an end. He wished Dan would consider staying around to help him and the rest of the company implement the four C's.

Marty had also shared with his wife last night what he was learning, and she was impressed with how simple yet powerful the model seemed. She, too, was now curious to find out what the fourth *C* would be and how it would fit into the model. Marty said, "I wish it wasn't our last day together; I've really learned a lot and feel I may fall short in executing on the four *C*'s. I feel like I could still use your help."

Dan eyed Marty seriously now and said, "Though you may not be perfect at them right away, the fourth *C* can buy you a lot of leeway and forgiveness from your team as you struggle to provide clarity, be more consistent, and remember to celebrate. The fourth *C* has what I like to call a multiplying effect on the other three *C*'s, meaning when this fourth *C* exists, even little improvements in clarity, consistency, and celebration can go a very long way. With the fourth *C* present, your team will recognize the efforts you're trying to make with the other three *C*'s. They'll give you credit, so to speak, for those efforts. May I?" Dan pointed to the whiteboard.

Marty was intrigued and felt a surge of energy pass through him as they jumped right in. "Of course," Marty said, raising his hand toward the board. "It's all yours."

Dan drew a big circle around the pyramid, and then he wrote the word *charity*. He stepped back from the board as if admiring it, then pointed to it. "This is the fourth *C*."

This is how it looked:

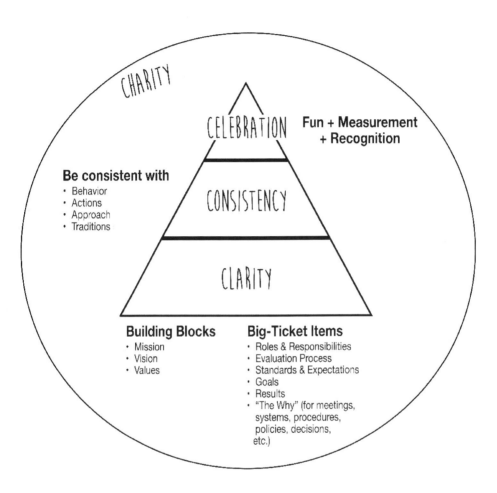

CHARITY

CELEBRATION   Fun + Measurement
              + Recognition

Be consistent with
• Behavior
• Actions
• Approach
• Traditions

CONSISTENCY

CLARITY

Building Blocks
• Mission
• Vision
• Values

Big-Ticket Items
• Roles & Responsibilities
• Evaluation Process
• Standards & Expectations
• Goals
• Results
• "The Why" (for meetings,
  systems, procedures,
  policies, decisions,
  etc.)

The Fourth *C*

Looking at the whiteboard at what Dan had just written, Marty was once again confused. *What does that mean?* he wondered. He first thought of charitable organizations and then of charitable contributions. This brought thoughts of free handouts and the American Red Cross and Salvation Army. None of this seemed to fit. *What does charity have to do with the other three C's, and how will it help me be a good boss?* Though he was confused, Marty knew there was always more.

"Charity is the last *C* in the four *C's* model to leadership success. Charity is about how people feel at work—whether they feel accepted, known, and respected," Dan explained. "It's whether they feel cared about as a person rather than an expendable object. Though this *C* is the most touchy-feely of them all, it's so important."

Marty was surprised by this. Like fun, making sure people felt cared for wasn't always something that was openly spoken about in the business world. As Dan had mentioned, he believed it was just too touchy-feely and very subjective. Most business-minded people Marty had worked with looked for hard numbers, facts, and data to help them succeed. Charity certainly didn't sound like this at all. And although intellectually Marty knew people needed to feel cared about, he still wasn't exactly sure what that looked like at work. "I'd really *care* to learn more," he said, emphasizing the word *care* and reviving the corny joke he'd made the first day they met.

Dan smiled and asked, "Of all the bosses you've had, which one would you say cared about you the most?"

Marty didn't hesitate long on this one. "Julie, for sure. Julie was my boss for a little over two years before the one I just left when I accepted this position here."

"That was quick," Dan said sounding surprised Marty was able to respond so quickly. "And why do you say Julie? What made you feel like she cared about you more than the others you've worked with?"

"She was always so supportive of me. I could just tell she genuinely was interested in me and my success." As Marty thought about it more, he did feel Julie cared about him, and that really mattered to him.

He looked up, and he could tell Dan wasn't completely satisfied with his response and wanted more. "How was she supportive, and how did you know she was really interested in your success?"

Marty thought about it for a few more seconds. "I don't know exactly. She just always seemed interested in me and knew how my projects were coming along. She always seemed to have time for me. She was genuine."

"Did Julie know anything about you outside work?" Dan asked as if he were still trying to get Marty to think this through and open up more.

"Oh yes, for sure," Marty said. "She frequently asked how my wife, April, was doing. She was always curious if she was feeling well during her pregnancy and always inquired about my daughter after she was born. She seemed very interested in my family because she always asked me how they were doing and what they were up to."

Marty paused and shrugged, then added, "She knew they were an important part of my life. In fact, most of my interactions with Julie started with an update on my family before we'd ever talk business."

Dan nodded as if giving approval for what Marty was sharing. "That's great. And it sounds a lot like Julie. I've actually gotten to know her over the years and really admire her as a colleague in our organization."

Though it should not have been too surprising, Marty didn't realize Dan knew Julie. She had been a part of the organization for about six years, but she wasn't "home grown" like Marty and many of the CEOs in the organization. She also wasn't one of the long-tenured leaders in the company like Dan.

Marty decided to share more. "Something else I liked about Julie was that she even took an interest in my personal interests. She knew very little about golf, for example, but she knew I tried to play most weekends. On Mondays she'd always ask how it went, if it was a nice day, and if I had played well. She wanted to know what my score was and asked why I wasn't improving." Marty smiled at that thought and added, "She was just always that way with most everyone who worked under her."

"And how did that make you feel?"

"Well, I certainly felt cared about, if that's what you mean," Marty responded.

Dan quickly added, "What impact, if any, did it have on your performance at work?"

"Oh, I'd do anything for Julie still to this day. In fact, if she called me right now and needed something, I'd have to excuse myself and help her. She's just that kind of person, and I have that much respect for her. I know she'd do the same for me." It slowly hit him what he was saying. Marty realized he probably wouldn't react the same to a request from most of his prior bosses. Sure, if they called and needed help, he'd eventually do it, but he wouldn't be excited about it and would probably do it grudgingly. But with Julie, he'd jump all over it. Marty noticed he already was beginning to buy into the importance of the fourth *C*.

"It sounds like Julie is an excellent example of what charity is all about," Dan said as he leaned back in his chair, interrupting Marty's thoughts.

Marty didn't have to think about that for more than a second to realize Dan was probably right.

"So charity," Dan said, "is making sure you help your people know you care about them as people. To establish this *C* within your team, you must get to know your people deeper than just on a superficial level. You should strive to learn their stories, what makes them tick, what interests they have outside work, and what they care most about. And once you know this, you can further strengthen charity among those you lead by responding to them in a way that shows you know these things about them."

Marty again understood how this seemed right on the surface, but he wanted to learn more. As if reading his mind again, Dan continued.

"There are a lot more ways you can show you have charity toward those you lead, Marty. Each of us has our own unique ways of going about this. There is certainly not a one-size-fits-all approach to this. Or to any of the elements of the model for that matter."

Marty had wondered about that.

"At the end of the day, charity is all about what's in your heart. Do you genuinely care about your people? You can't fake it. People know if you truly care or not."

Marty thought about that comment as Dan paused for a moment. He concluded that Dan was right. When people pretended to be concerned about you, you usually knew it wasn't sincere.

"Now this isn't always easy." Dan looked directly at Marty. "But you can't be a truly awesome boss and have an amazing culture within your team without establishing this fourth *C*. People must feel cared about and respected. They must feel a level of compassion and kindness. They must feel like valuable human beings at work."

Marty's thoughts went back to Julie again. He thought about what he could learn from her as it seemed she had helped everyone on her team feel cared for. Marty realized that, in a lot of ways, Julie seemed like more than just a boss to him. She was a mentor and even a friend.

Dan interrupted Marty's thoughts again. "As I said earlier, one of the most important ways to create feelings of charity is finding ways to get to know your people and what's going on in their lives. This is the best place to start."

Marty was thinking of ways he could do that when Dan went on. "As you begin to get to know your team, it will help them feel cared about; it will help them feel like they are known. It will help them feel charity.

"Even more important than this, however…" Dan paused as if to add effect to what he was about to say. "Getting to know your people will change you. As their leader, it will create within you a greater desire to have charity toward those you lead. When you know more about them, it is easier to view them as people."

Dan paused again, and Marty could tell he wanted all this to sink in. Marty thought about how showing charity could not only help others feel cared about but also encourage him to have even more of it.

"Though you may not believe me at this moment," Dan said with a big smile, "I'm really not a big philosopher. But I think the reason this happens is when you learn about people's lives, what they enjoy doing, what they worry about, and what their joys and struggles are in life, it makes them just like you. You recognize they have aspirations, worries, desires, likes, and dislikes—just like you. It humanizes them more, which I think is important for leaders. It's easy for us to sit in this office removed from our people and just see them as numbers rather than real human beings."

Dan paused again as if he were thinking. Marty considered what Dan was saying. It seemed sensible to believe that the more you got to know people, generally speaking, the more you cared about them.

Marty then remembered a colleague he'd had when he first started at Wiser Care. Though quite a bit older than Marty, they had hit it off almost instantly, and before long they were golfing together and spending time outside work together. Though their careers had taken them in different directions, they still kept in touch and tried to catch up with each other when they had the opportunity. Like Julie, Marty had considered this person a friend before they ever started golfing together. He thought about how he was more and more interested in his success as he got to know him better, and he was sure his colleague probably felt the same about him.

Dan again interrupted Marty's thoughts. "Can I tell you something else about Sandy?" He leaned forward in his chair.

"Of course," Marty responded, interested to know more about Sandy, a leader he had grown to have a lot of respect for.

"I already mentioned how she celebrated or recognized my efforts way back in the day and how that act of kindness gave me a huge desire to come back to Wiser Care, even though she never mentioned it."

Marty nodded, acknowledging he remembered.

"Well, there's more I'd like to share about how Sandy has impressed me over the years and taught me a lot about charity and about being a great leader and boss."

Marty was interested and looked at Dan to encourage him to continue but noticed Dan seemed a little hesitant. Marty wasn't sure why and was about to say something when Dan said, "I want you to know that I haven't shared this with many people." Marty noticed he hesitated again. "My youngest son had some serious medical complications when he was younger, which kept me away from work for a little bit."

Marty leaned forward in his seat. He had become so interested in Dan's personal stories and was curious where this one would lead.

"Though I tried to keep it as quiet as possible, word somehow must have spread about my son, who was admitted to the pedi-ICU down at Children's Hospital. Somehow, this news made its way to Sandy. And after a few days in the hospital, my wife and I received a much-appreciated care basket full of very needed nonhospital food." Dan said this with a big smile and a chuckle. "My son devoured those things."

Then he continued. "Along with the basket was a heartfelt note from Sandy. Not only was I surprised she knew about our situation, but also I was surprised she'd taken the time to find out where we were and send us such a nice note and basket. To me, this really showed she cared about me and my family and that she knew us. I wasn't just another leader in this growing organization. I was somebody Sandy knew about and cared about.

"As you can imagine, I definitely felt a lot of charity from Sandy toward me and my family that day. It was a very kind gesture."

Marty was impressed with this simple act of kindness and nodded slowly to show he understood how this was a good example of charity.

Dan continued. "Now, there's even more to this story because Sandy didn't stop there." Marty raised his eyebrows,

172

already impressed by what Sandy had done, considering the thousands of employees she had to worry about throughout the organization.

"A few weeks later, I received a phone call from her. I was with my son when she called, so I didn't answer or respond right away. It had been a particularly hard day for us. And though I was surprised to see she had called, I assumed she must be calling about something important at work. As I mentioned, it had not been a good day, and honestly, work was far from my thoughts at that time.

"Later that evening I did find the strength to pick up the phone and listen to the voice mail she'd left. I was sure it would lead to more phone calls and my dealing with something at work. Again, these were the thoughts that were going through my head."

Taking a breath, he added, "I couldn't have been more wrong. Rather than calling about work, Sandy had left a voice mail stating she was thinking about me, my son, and my family. She called to share she was hoping for all the best. She said the only purpose for her call was to check in on us and let us know she was thinking about us."

Marty leaned back in his chair, pretty impressed by what Dan was sharing.

"As you might guess, I was relieved to hear Sandy's message of care and concern rather than about work needs. And to be honest, though work had been far from my mind during these few weeks with my son, after Sandy's message, I felt a desire to get back to it and do more than ever to have success at Wiser Care."

Marty was impressed. Dan's story really began to solidify in his mind all he believed to be true about the CEO of their company.

"Now don't get me wrong," Dan continued, shaking his head a little. "I'm not saying everyone will have the same reaction or feelings I had at that time. Charity absolutely is not about doing things to get people focused on work. In fact, calling a colleague with a sick child in the hospital hoping it will make them want to return to work sooner is a bad idea. Remember, charity doesn't work that way. You can't fake it. If your intention is to get people to do something by showing kindness, it won't work very well in the long run. You must show kindness for kindness' sake. I could feel Sandy was sincerely rooting for me and my son."

Marty was again impressed. Though the company had been smaller back then, Sandy must still have been a very busy person, with responsibility for a lot of employees who worked at Wiser Care. To do that for Dan seemed above and beyond what anyone might expect from a busy corporate leader. Then Marty reflected back on how Sandy had treated his team after the success of the customer service initiative. Most of Marty's team were young and could have been viewed as pretty insignificant leaders in the organization at the time. Sandy could have easily ignored the results or simply assigned someone else to recognize the team. At that moment, Marty realized he felt Sandy cared about him and his family after that night. And like Dan, he walked away from that interaction with Sandy wanting to do more to not let her or the company down. Marty realized that on that evening Sandy had exhibited not only celebration but also charity as she seemed genuinely interested in getting to meet and know everyone in attendance. Marty felt he was understanding how the fourth *C* affected people at work and why it was important for successful leadership.

Exploring More

"Now, based on what you've told me about Julie, it sounds like you felt known, respected, and cared about; is that correct?" Dan asked, changing the subject and moving back to Julie. "You felt Julie saw you as a person with needs, interests, concerns, strengths, and weaknesses? You felt she saw you, in a way, as an equal; is that correct?"

Marty thought about what Dan was suggesting and said, "Yes, that's right. She never acted like she was better than me or tried to put me down. I think that's a big reason why everyone respected her. And she seemed to always be encouraging to all of us."

"Did she ever get after you, though? Like when you messed up?" Dan asked, looking seriously at Marty. "Was there ever a time when you didn't deserve a lot of charity?"

"Me, mess up?" Marty said, rolling his eyes as if what Dan had just suggested was something completely ridiculous.

Dan chuckled and said sarcastically, "I know what I'm asking may seem pretty far-fetched for someone as talented and as humble as you."

Marty's smile left, and his mouth opened in disbelief at what Dan had said in jest. "This coming from Mr. Perfect himself over there," Marty quipped. Both gentlemen laughed for a moment. Marty then said, "I can think of *one* time maybe where I messed up." He exaggerated the word *one* while holding up his index finger.

Dan, more serious now, said, "Tell me about it. What happened?"

Marty felt himself hesitate. Typically, he remained guarded and didn't share stories about his mistakes, but then he relaxed. Like Julie, he felt Dan's sincere interest in him as a leader. He could feel Dan truly wanted him to succeed, so he jumped right in.

"One day, Julie made it very clear to me that she wanted me to make sure our maintenance team replaced all the wheelchair arms in our center that had even the slightest tear in them. She told me this was a top priority and that the health examiners had been nailing other health care centers for wheelchair arms with tears because of the potential risk of spreading infection. She was clear on what she wanted," Marty said, now completely opening up.

"Well, when I went to find the maintenance director, he was in the middle of a routine A/C inspection. He said he'd be done in about an hour, so I told him I'd be back to chat with him about something important that needed to be taken care of ASAP. I had every intention of circling back with him but became so busy with other things that I completely forgot about it."

Marty noticed Dan was looking at him as if he was really listening and wanted to hear what happened next. He laughed to himself, thinking that this must be how he normally looked as Dan shared his personal stories of past mistakes. Marty went on.

"At the end of the day, as I was heading out the door, I ran into Julie, and she asked if all the wheelchair arms in the center had been replaced. I completely froze. Normally, I'm really on top of things, and I'm very good at remembering important items, but in the chaos of the day, I had somehow completely forgotten. I instantly felt two inches tall."

Marty noticed Dan lean forward and thought he must be really enjoying the story. He said, "All I could do was come clean and tell her what happened. I was so embarrassed and upset at myself for having made this mistake, and I could tell she wasn't very happy, either.

"She let me know she was serious about getting it done today and was disappointed I hadn't taken care of it like she'd asked. She then had me call the maintenance department to see who was still around to help with the project, stating it had to be done immediately for the care and well-being of our patients and staff. Needless to say, she and I stayed very late that night with some of the maintenance crew, and we took care of it. Julie never yelled, said unkind things, or even rolled her eyes when we messed up, but we always knew when we had disappointed her. I still hate thinking about that day because I knew I had let her down."

Dan raised his eyebrows, seeming impressed.

Marty added, "Of course, later that week during our one-on-one meeting, she shared with me how what had happened that day was unacceptable. She made it clear that she had to have leaders she could count on. She made sure I knew not to make the same mistake again." Marty shook his head and paused for a moment, reflecting back. Looking down he added, "She also expressed how she knew I had incredible potential and that she wanted to see me succeed. She pointed out that she knew my performance that day was uncharacteristic of the type of leader I was and even thanked me for all the good contributions I was making to the team."

The two colleagues sat in silence for a moment, then Dan, sounding sincere, said, "Thank you for sharing that. Julie is a great example of this fourth *C*, and let me tell you why." Again, Dan paused for a brief moment as if he wanted to make sure

Marty was listening. "Because she held you accountable in a kind way."

Marty was a little confused about what that meant but waited to see if Dan would continue.

Sure enough, Dan went on. "Too often, leaders confuse what this fourth *C* is all about. Though it has to do with kindness, concern for others, and respect, it's not about ignoring problems or not addressing issues. You can take any action in a kind and respectful way. This includes holding someone accountable or disciplining them or even terminating them. Charity is about caring about people so much that you'll do whatever it takes to help them succeed. It's not about avoiding confrontation or not addressing poor performance. It's just the opposite."

Marty had been wondering if charity was all "kumbaya" and trying to be "nicey-nicey" all the time. He wondered about how to apply it when there were real problems and when hard conversations were needed. He was relieved to know that charity was not about avoiding these things.

"If you care about someone, you're going to want them to progress and do well. Even if it means they aren't going to appreciate your honest feedback in the moment. Charity is about caring so deeply for those you lead that you'll do whatever it takes to help them, even if that means sharing negative feedback with them, letting them go from a job they're not succeeding at, or insisting they stay late to complete a missed assignment. It's telling them where they must improve, even when you know they'll be upset at you."

Dan again paused, and Marty could tell he wanted that to sink in. He knew how hard it was to address issues when you knew how the other person might react. Sometimes it was easier to brush things aside, hoping they might get better on their own. This rarely worked, however. Marty could see how ignoring problems wasn't really all that kind to the person.

"We can take any action with our people either with or without charity. The four *C's* model to successful leadership reminds us it is always best to do it with charity."

Marty reflected on that. He thought he got it, and he could see Dan waiting. Marty asked, "I think I understand, but can you give me an example?"

"Yes, absolutely." Dan looked like he was thinking for a moment. "Many years ago, when I was a young supervisor, I had an employee who stole money from one of our registers. She had been caught, and I was livid. I couldn't believe that any employee of ours would do such a thing. So I marched over to this person's work area and fired her on the spot in front of a few of her peers. I let her know how egregious I felt her actions had been and that she was never welcome to return to our health care center again."

Marty had a hard time picturing the Dan he knew now doing such a thing. He recognized that firing a person like that was not a professional or kind way to handle things, no matter how upset you might be.

"That was a mistake," Dan said. "I've replayed that termination in my head from time to time, and although stealing is a viable reason for letting someone go, I still feel guilty about how I handled myself that day."

Marty nodded in agreement.

"I've learned from my mistakes, though. About a year ago, we had a similar situation here. However, this time I sat down with the employee privately and let them know they would be terminated. I also took the time to listen to them as they apologized and shared that they were dealing with some real financial pressures. This person admitted they were feeling desperate and had made a very poor decision. I felt sorry for this individual, but I knew the termination was necessary to uphold our standards of zero tolerance on theft and remain consistent with how we've handled similar infractions in the past."

Marty certainly understood that. Dan added, "I believe the person felt much better having the chance to explain their situation and apologize. Can you see how these two similar situations were handled very differently?"

Marty nodded. He could definitely see the difference between the two. He thought about how each termination was handled and how they might have affected others who worked for Dan as well. Marty had learned that the way terminations were carried out at work was usually discussed among staff no matter how private a supervisor tried to make them.

Dan broke Marty from his thoughts. "So charity is not about avoiding certain actions we need to take. We can perform any action with or without charity. Charity is about taking action from a place where we have genuine concern for the person. The reality is that even terminating someone can be done with or without charity."

Marty thought that seemed right; he could see a clear example in Dan's termination stories. He had taken very different approaches to similar situations: one with charity and one without it.

"Let me share another termination story with you, if I can," Dan said. Before Marty could even respond, he continued. "Many years ago, here at this center, I had a department head who was really struggling in her role. Though I made efforts to help her, it never seemed to be enough. Soon she recognized she was struggling and not performing like I and the center needed her to. And, as is usually the case, the rest of the team recognized this person was not performing very well or living up to standards.

"I knew she was in over her head, but in an effort to establish what I thought was charity, I gave this department head chance after chance after chance. She sometimes would improve for a little while, but it never lasted long. We both struggled with her lack of consistent performance, and it affected our entire team. After a much longer time than I care to admit, I finally did end up terminating this employee."

Marty wondered where Dan was going with this story and didn't understand exactly how it related to charity. Rather than say anything, he assumed Dan would help him connect the dots.

"Within a few weeks, this employee entered my building while working for one of our vendors. I was surprised how happy and relieved she looked. I had a relationship with her supervisor, who was our account manager. During a meeting with him one day he commented how this person was such a great addition to their team. He said he was thrilled to have her onboard and felt she was really enjoying her job. After that, when I saw her from time to time as she entered our building to make a delivery, it was obvious she was so much happier at work. Over the years I've continued to watch this person do well in her role with this organization."

Marty still wasn't sure the point of the story and how it fit in. Just when he was about to ask, Dan added, "I hung on to this employee way too long, and she was miserable. She was negatively impacting her peers, and she knew it. She was suffering, being stuck in a job she wasn't succeeding in, and our center's results were suffering. In the supposed name of charity, I gave this leader chance after chance after chance, and this went on for months and months." Dan shook his head. Marty began to understand what this story had to do with the fourth C.

"Rather than helping this person, the truth was I was saving myself from the difficult task of letting someone I cared about go. I didn't want to take that action and tried to tell myself I was demonstrating charity." Dan was still shaking his head as if recalling his mistake. "So the point I'm trying to drive home is that charity is about caring so much for people that we do things that will most help them. And believe me, in the moment, this department head was furious that I had let her go, but it was the best thing I could have done for her. When people aren't succeeding, it's hard for them to enjoy their work. Sometimes people are just in the wrong position, and the kindest thing we can do is help them move on so they can find a better fit."

Marty was fascinated by what Dan was sharing. On the one hand, Dan had a reputation for being fiercely loyal to his staff, but on the other, he was also known for moving quickly when someone wasn't performing. Marty had silently wondered how that worked but now felt it was all beginning to become clear.

"Holding people accountable and helping them be successful, just as Julie did for you when you messed up, is an act of charity when done with the right intentions. How do you think things might have been different had Julie not mentioned anything to you and just taken care of it herself, for example?" Dan asked, pulling Marty away from his thoughts again.

Marty thought about it. "I suppose if Julie hadn't said anything to me, I might have felt many of the things she asked me to do weren't that important. This might have led me to develop bad habits like not taking action on items that needed to be taken care of." He paused. "I also maybe would have learned not to worry about holding people accountable myself if she had let me off the hook. I mean, I really looked up to her and learned a lot from her."

Marty stopped again, but he was still thinking. "Without her holding me accountable that day, I can see how a lot of negative things could have potentially come from it. But because she did,

I instead learned to be more responsible and follow through with what I commit to do. Most important, I learned from her example of how to hold people accountable in a kind way, as you said. This has made me a better leader and really a better person."

"I love it." Dan leaned forward and slapped the air above his head as if he was giving someone a high five. "I think you might be getting this after all. I was beginning to wonder if you ever would," he said with a smile, teasing Marty.

Marty smiled and shook his head, amused by Dan's comment.

Charity and the Model

After taking a quick break, the two sat back down in the chairs they'd become accustomed to sitting in over the last few days. After some small talk, Marty asked sincerely, "So tell me more how charity works with the other three C's in the model."

"I'm so glad you brought that up. As I mentioned earlier, charity acts like a multiplier or magnifier in the model, and that's why it encircles the other three C's. If you provide a lot of clarity, but people don't really know if you care about them or not, your clarity will go only so far in helping you build a cohesive team and healthy workplace culture. The clarity you create will always have a positive impact, but if you add charity to it, its impact becomes so much greater than it would be without it. The impact of that clarity is magnified. The two combined are a powerful force for enhancing your ability to be a transformational leader. The same is true when you add charity to consistency and celebration. The more charity your team feels from you and the organization, the bigger the impact the other three C's will have on those you lead."

Marty thought he understood what Dan meant but wondered if he should ask for some more concrete examples. He waited for just another moment, and it paid off.

"Let me try and share a simple example to better illustrate this point. Remember how I mentioned yesterday that I set a goal with our receptionist at the front desk to measure the number of smiles she got from those who walked through our door or passed by her desk? And that we decided to celebrate when she met her goal or broke her record?"

Marty did remember that and thought it was an interesting example of celebration. He still wanted to talk to his receptionist about it. He was grateful Dan had reminded him, and he took a quick note, responding, "Yes, of course."

"So our initial goal was fifty smiles. So let's just say a few days later, after working hard to get people to smile, she comes to my office excited and exclaims she did it. She got fifty people to smile in one day. Now it's time to celebrate, right?" Marty nodded, unsure of where Dan was going again.

"Now I'm thinking about how to celebrate her achievement, and I realize I don't know my receptionist very well at all." Dan paused for a moment. "This is only hypothetical," he said, trying to look innocent.

Marty had to laugh. "I'm sure it is," he said sarcastically, now teasing Dan.

"I promise you it is." Dan put both hands up in front of him and snickered.

"Anyway, hypothetically speaking," Dan said, appearing to regain his composure, "let's say I decide I'll celebrate with her by ordering her a pizza from the best pizza place in town, because who doesn't love pizza, right?"

Marty nodded. "Of course," he said, paying closer attention to Dan's example.

"Well, let's just say our receptionist is part of the small percent of the population who doesn't like it. Let's take it a bit further and say she not only doesn't like it but also is lactose intolerant and can't eat it. So it's not even an option for her for health reasons."

Marty noticed Dan pausing like he usually did when he wanted to make sure Marty understood. Marty felt like he knew now where Dan might be heading with this example and nodded to show he was listening.

"Of course, I have no idea about this because I haven't ever taken the time to get to know her. After all, she's just the receptionist." Dan said the last part sounding sarcastic, as if that would be a poor excuse for not getting to know her.

Marty thought he really liked that about Dan. He seemed to take interest in everyone at his center, regardless of their position. He realized this was probably partly a result of his focus on the four *C*'s model. To Marty, taking interest in people regardless of their position seemed like a way to further establish consistency and charity.

Dan moved forward in his chair now, looking right at Marty, pulling him away from his thoughts and grabbing his attention again. "Because there's a low level of charity in this situation, because I don't know anything about what she likes, nor do I seem interested in finding out, how much of an impact will this celebration have on her, do you think?"

"Not much, if any at all." Marty responded quicker than he had anticipated, adding, "In fact, she may feel a little upset you'd get her something she doesn't like and can't even eat. That would be annoying if not discouraging to me for sure."

"That is true. This will certainly show I don't know much about her. And I'm her boss," Dan said emphatically as if to illustrate the point that her boss should know her. "Now, knowing Michelle, I'm sure she might be kinder than that. I'm sure she might appreciate my effort and be grateful I followed through with at least something. With that being said, how motivating do you think my celebration was to her for the next time around?"

"Probably not motivating at all," Marty responded.

"You're probably right." Dan paused again as Marty thought about his example. He could certainly see how a lack of charity affected this act of celebration.

Dan then said, "Now let's say, instead, I had taken the time to get to know my receptionist. In fact, let's say I learned she absolutely loved popcorn. Instead of celebrating with pizza, I present her with nice bags of gourmet caramel and buttered popcorn that she can share with others. How much more meaningful would this celebration be?"

"I'm sure a lot more."

"And how much more motivated will she be the next time I set a goal with her?"

Marty nodded. "A lot more."

"I can tell you, you're right. She freaked out." Dan chuckled again as if recalling the memory.

Marty thought about this for a few moments. He realized the receptionist at the front had impressed him from the day he began as he observed her greeting everyone with a big welcoming smile. He understood now that, in part, this was because of the four C's. He was amazed how implementing the four C's had had such a big impact on both the receptionist and the level of customer service being provided in the front lobby. He then thought about how the four C's were probably having a significant impact on all the results in the building.

Dan continued. "I know this is a very simple example, but can you begin to see how charity has a multiplying effect on the other three C's? Anything you do to create clarity, improve consistency, and celebrate will improve your effectiveness as a leader. However, when high levels of charity exist, the impact these other three C's have on your team is significantly multiplied."

At that moment, Marty was so impressed with Dan's model. Though he knew he still had more to learn, as he looked over at the whiteboard, he could feel the implications it could have on his leadership and his results. He could see how each element of the model complemented the others. He was also beginning to see how missing even one could slow down the overall impact a leader had on his team.

Marty decided that, though the fourth *C* was more touchy-feely, he couldn't deny the powerful impact it had on others.

"Can I ask you something I asked about earlier?"

"Yes, of course," Marty responded, wondering what it might be.

"You mentioned earlier that Julie would do anything for you and that you knew she cared about you, but remind me how you knew."

Marty sat for a few seconds, thinking about it. He then said, "Like I mentioned earlier, she just seemed to care. She always showed interest in me, my family, and my personal interests outside work. I felt she cared about my success because she took the time to meet with me regularly. She'd offer help when I needed it, and she seemed like a true mentor. I assume that's why I just knew."

"I like that," Dan said. "You see, great leaders love the people they lead, and their people can feel it. People can tell how you feel about them."

Dan paused for another moment, then said, "If you're a boss and don't love the team you lead or the place where you work, you need to figure out a way to get there quickly. And if you can't, you probably should really find someplace where you can. A leader needs to believe in their team more than anyone else. For the team to truly embrace you as a leader and for you to be an enduring leader for those you lead, you must have charity."

Marty thought about this. He knew a lot of leaders he didn't think cared much for their teams. He realized, too, that personality conflicts and egos probably played roles in this. But no matter the reason, he was sure none of these leaders got 100 percent from their teams as a result.

"Charity is simple, Marty. It doesn't require you to do big or extravagant things. You can show kindness and concern best through simple acts. Remember the one-minute phone call from Sandy when my son was sick or the patience from Julie when you messed up."

Marty hadn't considered this much. Though he wasn't necessarily thinking he had to do huge things to demonstrate charity, he also hadn't considered how simple it could be. He could see how simple, sincere acts of kindness seemed to be at the heart of charity.

His thoughts then turned to the small teams and departments he had led in the past. He felt in a lot of ways he did, indeed, have charity toward them. He certainly cared about them and felt he had always wanted the best for them. He knew charity was probably something that had helped him thus far in his career, and he hoped his charity could grow for the new team he was now responsible for leading. Based on their discussion this morning, Marty felt he had a pretty good idea of how to do it.

Getting Late

"Well, it's later than I thought," Dan said, looking at his watch.

Marty was surprised and looked at the clock on his wall. Dan was right.

"Thanks once again," Marty said, truly meaning it and sad the time had gone by so fast. "I've really learned a lot these last four days and wish our conversations could continue all throughout the day. I worry I'm such a novice at applying this model."

"Don't be so hard on yourself. I know you've been doing many of these things already without realizing it. Leaders are successful because, in some measure, they implement the four C's whether they understand the model or not. Without the model, though, too many leaders either fail to focus on the things that can help them be most effective or fail to realize what has made them successful in the first place. Remember how I stopped being consistent?"

Marty remembered Dan's story about consistency and how it had affected his team. He also remembered Dan saying he felt if he'd had the model, he might not have made such a big mistake because he would have been focusing on it.

Dan furrowed his brow now, looking over Marty's shoulder.

"Is something wrong?" Marty asked.

"Leadership isn't easy. It is extremely difficult. And though the ideas or elements within the model are simple to understand, they are not easy to implement. It takes a lot of effort. Believe me when I tell you it is not easy to provide clarity, be consistent, celebrate, and act with charity all the time. Some leaders do these things more naturally, whereas others must concentrate on them more. You can probably guess which type of leader I am based on all of my stories of past mistakes." Dan smiled widely. "The four *C*'s model will challenge you; it challenges every leader. It requires conscious daily effort on any leader's part."

Marty nodded as he believed it was true.

"One of the beauties of the model is that it can help all leaders—even those who are very different from one another. What I mean is you don't have to establish clarity, consistency, celebration, and charity the exact same way I did. It is designed to be flexible and can be adapted to any situation. Different teams, circumstances, and even industries may demand that a leader find unique ways to establish each of the *C*'s. The important part is striving to establish them among your team."

Marty was so glad for what Dan had just said. He had worried that he'd need to do the exact same things Dan had done to establish the four *C*'s. He realized now that different leaders could establish them in their own way, and that was OK. Marty felt more at ease knowing he didn't need to replicate every single thing Dan did to sustain them.

Dan broke Marty from his thoughts. "Understand also that this model is not a quick fix. It requires daily effort. The need for establishing clarity, consistency, celebration, and charity never goes away. It is always there. Sure, at the beginning establishing the *C*'s requires more diligent effort, but that doesn't mean you can abandon them and not face consequences. In a way, following the model is a lifelong pursuit for every leader. The more the *C*'s are established, the stronger your culture and results will be, and the more they are neglected or forgotten about, the weaker your culture and results will be."

Marty again felt a wave of appreciation for Dan. "I'm truly grateful for the knowledge you've shared with me the last couple of days. I know I will be a better leader because of it."

"It's really my pleasure," Dan said. "Leaders face so many distractions that can pull them away from doing the most important things. It can be hard to become a highly successful leader when you lack the four C's model to guide you. With the model in place, it can help direct your decisions and actions. With any decision, a leader should ask, 'Will this help me increase and reinforce the four C's or take away from the four C's?' Having this model laid out like this"—Dan motioned toward the whiteboard—"will help you increase your focus on all four. And this will help you become a truly great boss. With this model, I'm convinced any leader can have a lot of success under any circumstances, within any organization. It's simply about establishing each C with the team you lead."

Marty sat back and soaked it all in. He knew Dan was right, and his results spoke for themselves. Dan appeared relaxed.

"I'm really going to miss our morning meetings," Marty responded, and he meant it. "And I will do my best at implementing the model, though I have to admit that following you is a little daunting."

"You're a lot further along with the model than you realize," Dan said reassuringly. "Besides, I'm just a phone call away, and Grace, the CEO at the health care center just across town, is probably better at this than I am. She really did an excellent job in establishing the four C's pretty quickly with her team over there and turned that place around. I know she'll be happy to help you out as well. In fact..." Dan began to stand. "I'll introduce you two sometime soon. She'll be a great resource and help whenever you need it."

"Thank you," Marty responded. He had heard a lot about Grace, and knowing she knew about the model, he was dying to meet her. He recalled she was someone who had worked under Dan at his center for a few years. He realized the mentoring she received working under him had certainly paid off as she had turned a center that was really struggling for many years into a flagship center for the organization. In many ways it rivaled Dan's as one of the best in the entire company over the last couple of years. *Dan really is the man,* Marty thought, realizing he not only ran an amazing center but also had helped others such as Grace to do the same. Marty was again blown away by Dan's willingness to pass on his knowledge even if it might mean other centers' results may surpass his own.

"No problem," Dan said sincerely. "Now that I've written all over your whiteboard, why don't I come back tomorrow and actually show you a few things around the building and give you some inside information on a few of your people and a few of the challenges we've been working on? It will probably make everyone happy for us to actually begin doing some real work around here," Dan said jokingly.

"I would love that!" Marty responded a little too enthusiastically. He felt his cheeks turn red, and Dan laughed again. Marty then stood to shake Dan's hand.

"In the meantime, I think your nice picture here has inspired me to schedule a tee time. I look forward to seeing you again tomorrow." With that, Dan opened the door and was off.

***

After feeling elated that Dan would be returning tomorrow, the rest of Marty's day was busy. Throughout it, he tried to do things he thought might begin the process of establishing charity with his team, and it seemed to be already paying off.

For example, he found out some fun facts about a few of his key leadership team members, including his assistant, Kate. He also spent lunch in the employee break room in hall three getting to know some of the staff who worked the floor on that wing. When someone pulled the fire alarm on that unit later that afternoon, it was so much easier to give instructions to people he felt like he knew on a more personal level. He also felt they took directions better having gotten to know him some.

When Marty arrived home late that evening, he told April what the fourth *C* was and how it fit into the model. Like Marty, she couldn't believe it. She agreed with him that the model seemed brilliant and that each element was much needed in the workplace. Both could see how embracing each *C* would help any leader be successful. Though Marty realized it would be impossible to truly measure their impact, all four of the *C*'s just felt right to him. He knew they'd help him become an awesome boss.

Friday Surprise

Marty could see the street lights still on outside his office window, though it was obvious by the color of the sky that dawn was now fast approaching. He had gotten to the office earlier than normal because he'd had trouble sleeping the night before. This wasn't unusual for him, especially when he had ideas running through his mind like cars on a racetrack. Though his mind was focused on a lot of things, what kept coming back to him were the C's, which filled him with both excitement and some nervousness. He was excited because he could see how the four C's would really help him be a more successful leader but a little nervous that he had to follow the founder and creator of them.

Now that Dan had finished sharing his four C's model, Marty wasn't sure what to expect from him today. Since he couldn't sleep, he headed to work early knowing he'd be spending time with Dan. He had decided it was worth trying to get caught up on a few things before Dan arrived.

Sometime later, while Marty was in the middle of reviewing a labor report, Dan opened the door with his typical smile and expression of enthusiasm, waving his arm quickly as if motioning that he wanted Marty to follow him. Before Marty could say a word, Dan yelled across the office. "Hurry, Marty, come with me. I want to show you something."

Marty got up from his desk. He couldn't help but wonder where they were headed and what was going on. As he walked past his assistant's desk, following behind Dan, he noticed she wasn't there, which seemed strange. They turned left down the hallway, passing the offices and desks of many of his department heads. He noticed they were all empty too. *Where is everyone?* he thought to himself as he peered at his watch. *Normally, people are here by now.*

Marty continued to follow Dan, who was walking quickly ahead of him. As they got farther down the hall, Marty began hearing people laughing and chatting, and suddenly the smell of fresh pancakes hit him. "What is going on?" he asked Dan just before they entered the conference room.

"Surprise!" everyone yelled, and some blew noisemakers, which caused a few in the room to instinctively grab for their ears and laugh. They also doused Marty and Dan with confetti as they entered the room. "What's all this?" Marty asked, genuinely surprised. "Who is this for?"

"We wanted to celebrate your arrival at our center as our new boss," Kate said with a smile.

"Thank goodness Dan is finally leaving," another person chimed in from somewhere in the back of the room, and they all began to laugh. Some patted Dan on the back, reassuring him it wasn't true, even though everyone knew it was only a joke.

"Hey, I'm still here, and it probably isn't too late for Marty to change his mind about all this, so you better be careful about what you say," Dan responded, trying to say it with a straight face as everyone laughed again.

Marty looked around the room, amazed. The place was decorated, and there were pancakes and toppings, balloons, party favors, hats, and even a handmade sign that appeared to have signatures on it and read, "Welcome Marty to the Best Place to Work." The team had thought this one out, and Marty did feel welcome. What surprised him even more was that each person seemed to be genuinely interested in one another and happy to spend time together. From experience, Marty knew this was rare in the workplace—especially in health care, where budgets were always tight, the atmosphere often was heavy, time was money, and stress levels could be through the roof. Marty decided he could get used to celebration and the other C's.

***

Marty had a great time with his team that morning, and by the end of the day, he could honestly say he'd had some of the most fun at work he'd had in a very long time. He also felt remarkably connected to his new staff already.

To top his day off, Grace from the health care center on the other side of town stopped by late in the afternoon to welcome Marty, and they had a great discussion about the four C's. After hearing some of Grace's stories, Marty was even more convinced the four C's model was exactly what he needed to help him succeed as a leader.

Saturday

It was early Saturday afternoon, and though he'd thought he might be exhausted, Marty was feeling enthusiastic about his new responsibilities, health care center, and team. He was behind and would probably need to work some additional weekends to catch up, but he was so appreciative of Dan's time. Dan had come into the office that morning as well. He said he had a hunch Marty would be there and happened to be driving by the center on his way to a golf course. Dan joked with Marty that he just had to rub it in a little bit. Despite it being a slightly crisp, beautiful autumn day outside, the funny thing was, Marty didn't feel even a bit of jealousy. He thought this could be due only to the thrill of the challenges that were ahead of him and the path that had been laid out by Dan. The four *C*'s model drawn up on the whiteboard would stay there for a long time, Marty thought, to remind him of what he needed to focus on most.

Marty walked the halls of the health care center late Saturday afternoon and recognized signs of the four *C*'s all over. First, there was the wall on the far end of the corridor next to the break room with the nice decals listing the center's core values, providing clarity to the entire team about what the center stood for and what they hoped to represent. Then there was the task list on his assistant's desk, which she faithfully completed each day. To Marty, this was a symbol of the incredible consistency and discipline the entire team seemed to have. This brought him a feeling of security, knowing he could count on her and others. Next, there were the now-sagging helium balloons hanging from outside Marty's office door as well as the welcome sign that was now in his office, reminding him of the celebration he and his team had had the other day to welcome him as their new boss. Finally, there was the "Welcome New Hires" board in their main corridor with pictures and introductions of all the new staff who had joined the team during the month, including his own picture. This, to Marty, was an illustration of charity and communicated a powerful message to the new staff members that they belonged, were cared about, and were known.

Then Marty remembered the first day he'd met Dan. He had come in with Roger the housekeeper, who seemed like an old friend of his. He could tell Dan knew him well on a personal level, more than just what went on at work. He could tell they genuinely cared about each other. As Marty thought about it, he decided this was perhaps the best illustration of charity he had observed during all his years at Wiser Care.

Marty was surprised that he hadn't recognized some of these physical manifestations of the four C's before, even though he didn't know the model. What Marty did know back then, however, was from the moment he walked in the door of this health care center, he could feel an incredible vibe and good feeling that just seemed to permeate the building. It felt like no other health care center he had ever been to. Though he recognized this distinct feeling at the time, he wasn't sure what it was. Thanks to Dan and his team, he was now beginning to understand. This was going to be a challenge, indeed, following in the footsteps of a legend, but Marty knew he now had the model he needed to do it. He had the understanding of the four C's model to leadership success. He knew how to be an awesome boss!

Epilogue

Leadership Today

Organizations are desperate for good leaders who will manage their business and their teams well. And employees are desperate to work for a good boss. No longer is it enough to simply be smart or work hard. Leaders today have to be more than just smart and strategic in their approach. They must create an incredible work environment that attracts and retains the best talent. The four C's is a model that every leader can use to do this. Establishing clarity, building consistency, creating celebration, and demonstrating charity will separate the best leaders and organizations from the rest.

Applying the four C's will make you a leader others want to work for and organizations want working for them. Learning and striving to develop clarity, consistency, celebration, and charity as a leader will help you flourish in the increasingly competitive marketplace.

Organizational Health

The four C's is not only a model for being a transformational and enduring leader but also the way to structure and develop a strong organizational culture. Any organization that can create clarity, be consistent, find ways to celebrate, and build charity for team members will develop a strong and healthy culture that will produce exceptional results.

I've seen these principles applied in many different organizations and at many different levels. No matter the size, location, or type of business, time and time again, the four C's model has always produced an environment that encourages people to thrive and take pride in the services and products they deliver. If an organization is struggling—or even if it is doing well but would like to achieve more superior results—applying the four C's model will help it reach its potential.

Beyond the Workplace

The power of the four *C*'s goes beyond the walls of the workplace. Whether you are a parent, community organizer in charge of a volunteer group, or simply managing your own life, implementing the four *C*'s will help you find success. Creating clarity, being consistent, celebrating even in your personal life, and having charity will help you have better outcomes and results. Applying these simple principles in any situation will make your life better.

A Closer Look at the Model

There is tremendous satisfaction in becoming a successful leader and building a healthy organization using the four *C's* model. Though Dan shared with Marty how the four *C's* could help him become an awesome boss within his health care center, the four *C's* can apply at any level of any organization. The four *C's* is the model for not only great leadership but also building a healthy workplace culture that will have a dramatic impact on the results of any organization.

Clarity

Clarity is about making things as clear as possible throughout your organization and is at the base of the model. Without clarity, the other *C's* in the pyramid will struggle to influence a culture and organization like they should.

Most important, a leader or an organization should strive to create clarity around their mission, vision, and values. However, the more clarity created in an organization in general, the better off it will be.

The most common error when it comes to creating clarity happens when leaders and organizations believe they have been clear when they really haven't. Remember, someone has to hear something at least seven times before they really start to understand it, internalize it, and believe it. Repetition is key.

Consistency

As Dan pointed out, consistency is clarity in action. It is reinforcing the clarity with action. It is having the discipline to do what you say you are going to do. Consistency from a leader provides a feeling of dependability at work and something people can count on.

Consistency is also strengthened with traditions and norms in the workplace. Organizations should strive to create their own unique ways of doing business through traditions and consistency.

Remember, consistency is not about avoiding change. Organizations have to change and grow in order to stay relevant and be successful. Change is a necessity. So consistency is not about avoiding change but rather about how the organization handles and approaches change. If you can build consistency around your approach and response to change, people will feel much better about the frequent changes that inevitably will occur.

And all this consistency will lead to a sense of security. When people feel secure at work, when they know at some level what to expect day in and day out, week in and week out, year in and year out, they will want to stay. When organizations lose consistency, people can feel they are in an unpredictable situation. As humans, we love to feel we are on stable ground, so people may choose to go elsewhere when things are inconsistent. Again, this isn't about avoiding change. It's about how you act, behave, and implement change. If it's done consistently, change won't diminish the level of security that exists within the organization, and change won't be a thing to fear or run away from.

Celebration

Everyone needs to know what the goals and standards are within the organization; this is part of clarity. However, once goals are met, there needs to be celebration. Celebration is recognition plus measurement plus fun.

Celebration should not only happen when goals are met but leaders should celebrate progress and even small wins along the way. Measuring progress toward goals and making that progress super clear will allow leaders and organizations ample opportunity to celebrate and recognize performance at work.

All human beings have a need to be recognized. Though we may all like to receive recognition in different ways, the idea of being recognized for our efforts and work is important.

Celebrations are at the heart of happy and lasting memories for most of us. So much of what we do and look forward to in life centers around celebrations. So why not celebrate at work?

Celebrations foster an environment for deeper relationships. Humans have a need for connection with others. Many relationships within the work environment are on only a surface level. Thus, coworkers and colleagues feel little obligation to one another; there is no real connection. However, when celebrations bind people together, we feel connected and don't want to let each other down. Celebrations will create shared memories and stronger emotional ties to your organization and team.

Celebration is like the icing on the cake of a great culture. Without it, leaders and organizations miss an opportunity to strengthen their culture. The bottom line is, when people feel like their organization is good at celebration, they'll want to continue working there.

Charity

Charity is all about feeling cared about and known at work. Do people care about me as a human being, or is my boss or my employer solely interested in what I am able to produce? This is the question people will want to know from you and your organization. Are they expendable, or are you going to stick with them, get to know them, and believe in their unique value and contribution? When people feel known, respected, and cared for, their ability and desire to be productive and give their best become instinctive. When people feel unappreciated, disrespected, and not known, their performance will always be less than what it could otherwise be.

Charity is a multiplier of the other three C's within the model. Without it, the initial three C's will help but will go only so far. With it, and a high level of it, the other three C's will create a powerful culture that can transform any organization. The multiplying impact of charity is real.

As Dan pointed out, sometimes well-intentioned leaders misunderstand charity and believe it encourages them to avoid confrontation or taking action on poor performance. Or in other words, charity allows you to not hold people accountable in the name of being kind. This couldn't be further from the truth.

First, not helping people perform well and ignoring their mistakes are not acts of kindness. They simply set people up for failure, which is very unkind. Second, a leader can perform any act with or without charity. A leader can celebrate with or without charity, they can terminate the employment of someone with or without charity, and they can interview someone with or without charity. It is not about the action but rather about our way of being during that action. It's when we have charity that the impact of the actions we take will result in the most favorable outcomes, independent of the actions themselves.

Will charity make everything perfect? Of course not. When you act with charity, will people never get upset or feel slighted, unhappy, or disgruntled? Of course not. But it will keep those negative emotions and feelings as low as they possibly can be, and this will benefit the leader and the organization.

Remember, charity is about how a leader and organization view people and whether they see them as they see themselves. Do they view and treat people as people or as objects? People can tell whether true charity exists in an organization (or in a leader). You can't fake it.

The Four *C*'s

The four *C*'s work together and build on each other. They support each other. Trying to determine if an action or behavior will help establish one *C* or another is not always possible as there are many things leaders and organizations do that may help reinforce and establish two or three or all four at once. An annual celebratory leadership trip to Costa Rica each time company goals are met, for example, could help establish not only celebration but also consistency, clarity, and charity. Know that trying to isolate one specific element and establish it without influencing others is nearly impossible. Again, each element builds on and supports the others, and there are actions and systems leaders can take to help promote and establish all four.

Remember, anything you do to create clarity, consistency, celebration, and charity will help you as a leader and an organization. On the flip side, anything you do that takes away or diminishes clarity, consistency, celebration, or charity will hurt your results.

Whether you are a front-line supervisor, run your own small business, are in charge of a large division, or lead a corporation, applying the four *C*'s model will help you become a transformational and enduring leader.

Acknowledgments

Where do you begin when you have so many people who have shaped your understanding, thought process, character, and career? How do you list the hundreds, even thousands of people who have in some way touched or influenced your life and have shaped this book in some small way? It is hard to know where to start.

I'd like to thank first and foremost my wife. Lisa, you've been my cheerleader, coach, wise adviser, and friend. Throughout this crazy process you've been there to challenge my thoughts, question my stories, push me to improve it, and finally give me your undying support that this project was worth it and needed to be completed. Thank you!

I'd like to thank two of my good friends who took the time out of their very busy schedules to collaborate with and help me: Rico Maranto and Eric Gillis. Your insights were invaluable. Thank you for helping with this project and being mentors and examples of great leadership.

I need to thank my kids, who put up with a dad who was locked away in his home office for many hours when all they wanted was to play, get a ride, or talk. I only hope I can apply the four *C*'s model effectively in our home so you can benefit from having a good father.

My parents have always been instrumental in my life and have supported me in just about anything I've chosen to do. They've shaped my thought process and understanding as a leader more than anyone else has. Thanks for always providing clarity, consistency, celebration, and charity in my life.

Thanks to my siblings and their spouses for their unwavering support and input. The steady force our family offers in all things I do is such a blessing in my life.

I would be remiss if I didn't thank the several editors, designers, and others who have helped with the creation of this book. Your own personal touch and improvements have been priceless.

I need to thank God for His grace and kindness to a very imperfect soul. Throughout this process I felt Your guiding hand and influence.

Finally, to all who I have had the privilege and honor to work alongside throughout my career and life. To name all of you would be completely impossible, but you know who you are. Thank you for teaching me what it takes to be an awesome boss!

About the Author

Tim Burningham is founder and president of The Center for Company Culture, a management consulting firm specializing in organizational culture and leadership development. As an experienced manager, leader, and CEO, Tim has real-life experience leading multiple teams in a competitive work environment. He has helped many organizations gain a competitive advantage through building a healthy workplace culture. Tim's practical, simple, straightforward approach has helped leaders and organizations tackle some of their biggest challenges, such as employee retention and engagement, leadership, teamwork, and more.

Tim lives in the Houston area with his wife, Lisa, and their five children.

To learn more about Tim and The Center for Company Culture, please visit www.TheCenterforCompanyCulture.com or connect with him on LinkedIn.

The Center for
Company Culture

The Center for Company Culture is dedicated to helping organizations accelerate their results through effective leadership and creating a strong and healthy culture. To learn more about our products and services, please visit our website at TheCenterforCompanyCulture.com.

For more information about *The Four C's Model to Leadership Success*, please contact Tim at Tim@TheCenterforCompanyCulture.com.

You can also learn more at **BeAnAwesomeBoss.com**.

Made in the USA
Las Vegas, NV
06 August 2021

27697174R00125